DATE DUE

D1791848

GOLDEN GATE SEMINARY LIBRARY

THE GOLDEN CALF
and the Origins of the anti-Jewish Controversy

SOUTH FLORIDA STUDIES IN THE HISTORY OF JUDAISM

Edited by
Jacob Neusner
William Scott Green, James F. Strange

Number 16
The Golden Calf
and the Origins of the anti-Jewish Controversy

by
Pier Cesare Bori

THE GOLDEN CALF
and the Origins of the anti-Jewish Controversy

by

Pier Cesare Bori

translated by
David Ward

literary editor
Caroline McCracken-Flesher

Scholars Press
Atlanta, Georgia

THE GOLDEN CALF
and the Origins of the anti-Jewish Controversy

©1990
University of South Florida

Publication of this book was made possible by a grant from the Tisch Family Foundation, New York City. The University of South Florida acknowledges with thanks this important support for its scholarly projects.

Library of Congress Cataloging in Publication Data

Bori, Pier Cesare.
    [Vitello d'oro. English]
    The golden calf, and the origins of the anti-Jewish controversy /
by Pier Cesare Bori ; translated by David Ward.
    p. cm. -- (South Florida studies in the history of Judaism ;
16)
    Translation of: Il vitello d'oro.
    Includes bibliographical references (p.) and index.
    ISBN 1-55540-551-7
    1. Bible. O.T. Exodus XXXII--Criticism, interpretation, etc.--History. 2. Golden calf (Bible)--History of doctrines.
3. Judaism--Controversial literature--History and criticism.
4. Christianity and antisemitism. I. Title. II. Series.
BS1245.2.B6713
222'.12064--dc20   90-19125
                                             CIP

Printed in the United States of America
on acid-free paper

Table of Contents

Foreword vii
Introduction: In the Absence of Moses 1
I. The Original Sin of the People 9
II. Jewish Carnality 27
III. In the Church 55
Conclusions 73
Appendix I: The Golden Calf in the Biblical Tradition and in the
    Koran 85
Appendix II: Images and Stereotypes of the Jewish People in the
    Ancient World: Golden Ass, Golden Calf 101
Abbreviations 115
Bibliography 117
Index 123

Foreword

The Golden Calf took its origin from a seminar held in Tantur, near Jerusalem, at the Ecumenical Institute for Advanced Theological Studies, in 1975. The topic was "The Anti-Judaism of the Church Fathers and the New Testament." My work developed over subsequent years and became the book published by Boringhieri, Turin, in 1983.

The English translation contains in addition, in Appendix II, my essay *Golden Ass, Golden Calf* (1989), which gave me the opportunity to return to the subject and to examine it from another complementary point of view.

All translations of quoted texts are my own, even when not explicitly indicated.

P.C.B.

Introduction

In the Absence of Moses

In the absence of Moses:

> The glory of the Lord dwelt upon Mount Sinai and the cloud covered it for six days. On the seventh day the Lord called Moses from the cloud. The glory of the Lord appeared to the eyes of the Israelites as a devouring fire on the mountain top. Moses then entered the cloud, and went up the mountain, and there remained for forty days and forty nights (Exod. 24: 16-17).

Here the story stops. We are told, however, that inside the cloud the Lord spoke to Moses, gave him sacerdotal instructions and, lastly, "passed him the two tablets of the Tokens, tablets of stone, written by the finger of God" (31:18). But, in the mean time, what was happening below?

> The people, seeing that Moses was late, gathered around Aaron and said to him: "Make us *elohim* to walk in front of us, for we do not know what has become of that man Moses who brought us out of the land of Egypt." And Aaron said to them: "Strip the gold ear-rings from the ears of your women, your sons and your daughters, and bring them to me." And all of the people stripped themselves of the ear-rings they wore on their ears, and took them to Aaron. And Aaron took them from their hands and cast them into a mould, and made of it the image of a calf. And they said: "These are your *elohim*, Israel, that brought you out of Egypt." And Aaron saw, and built an altar in front of it, and exclaimed: "Tomorrow, the feast of God." And the next day they rose early and offered holocausts, and brought communion sacrifices: and the people sat down to eat and drink, and got up to amuse themselves (32: 1-6).

God now warns Moses: "Go down, Moses, for your people, who you brought out of Egypt, have strayed. Immediately, they have deserted the path I ordered them to follow...I have seen this people, they are a stubborn people of slow minds. Now I shall vent my anger and devour them, and I shall make of you a great people." In response, Moses pleads with God and reminds him of his commitments. God consequently abandons his plans (32: 11-14). Now Moses climbs down the mountain, sees the calf and the revelry, angrily breaks the tablets, smashes the calf into dust and powder, and sprinkles it on the water, which he then forces the Israelites to drink. He admonishes Aaron and unleashes the revenge of the sons of Levi: three thousand people are put to death (32: 25-28). Then once again Moses prays to God (32: 30-31; 33: 12-17). He reascends Mt. Sinai with two new tablets; the Lord takes his place beside him (34: 1-8) and again gives him the commandments (prohibition of idolatry, the sabbath, feasts, first born children, sacrifices). The commandments are then written on the tablets (34: 10-28). Finally, Moses climbs down the mountain, his face shining with glory (34: 29-35).

These are the events. Even as we summarize them, and still more as we return to the text for a closer reading, two considerations become apparent to us. Firstly, the biblical story presents many points which are not immediately self-evident – interruptions in the narrative, repetitions, contradictions, obscure terminology – and that require recourse to specialized exegesis if we are to clarify them. But secondly and above all, whatever the specialists may say, the collection of the narrated events is unmistakably clear. In the context of biblical history these are events of the greatest urgency; they constitute Israel's betrayal at the very moment, one might say, in which it is chosen to enter into the covenant with God. A "no" immediately follows a "yes," for the people cannot tolerate the absence of Moses, their guide.

It is surprising, on reflection, that the Bible, the national book of that people that is here for the first time accused, should so fearlessly record this memory. The sharp contrast between received benefits and transgression is such that even the story of original sin, confined as it is to the primordial backwoods of myth, pales when its tone and detail are compared to the circumstantiated cruelty of the narration of the first apostasy of Israel.[1]

Postponing a consideration of the exegetic aspects to a later separate analysis, I would like here to dwell on the centrality of this event in the biblical context.[2] Situated after the covenant on Mt. Sinai and the gift of the decalogue, it both presupposes and manifests in a clear light the foundations of Old Testament revelation. It posits Monotheism, which demands both the confession of the single God and the renunciation of any representation of him; Creation, according to

---

[1] See Barth (1953) p. 470 ss.
[2] For exegetic aspects, see Appendix I.

which God is not in the world, and yet the world stands before him as one of his creatures, not opposed to him as an autonomous and contrary principle; Revelation, through which God, who is unknowable, makes himself present and communicates his will to man; Election, by which one people among many is chosen as witness to God's self-revelation; Covenant, according to which God and the people of Israel – separate realities, as are God and the world – commit themselves to a reciprocal faith, manifested through coherent behaviour. It posits also Mediation – charismatic and prophetic figures, beginning with Abraham, appear throughout the Bible and underline that direct access to the divinity (the Bible does not represent a mystic way) comes about through the experience of men chosen not for their individual merits but by divine initiative, a privilege that often costs them their lives. And it posits Sin, whose capital form – idolatry – is not so much the abandoning of the one and only God and his name in order to follow other gods (although it is also this), as the giving of the name of God to that which he is not (in the case of Exod. 32, to the golden calf, a symbol of power and fertility celebrated in the name of the one and only God, indeed a symbol on which Israel states it will base its own trust in itself and in its vital energies). Finally, the law, already laid out in its essential form in the decalogue (Exod. 20), is broadened after the fall by way of more detailed prescriptions on worship (Exod. 34 and other entire books of the Bible) until it envelops the entire existence of the people within its tight web so that no act can escape its discipline.

Regardless of whether one judges these enunciations as truth or perversion of the originary revelation, their importance, which the golden calf episode contains and manifests, becomes yet more evident when compared to successive developments which speak of a New Testament and of a Jewish/Christian revelation. In Christian circles, none of these enunciations is lost, but equally none remains the same. Creation, revelation, election, mediation, sin, law – all are present. But here, while always entailing the original meaning, they take on a different value in the presence of the mediator, he who is believed to be absolute and definitive, the Messiah who has come and is awaited again at the end of time. Thus, for example, idolatry will no longer be betrayal through the making of images, but betrayal of the single image of God, the man Jesus. And fidelity, or faith, will be measured against both the conformity of this image and all the ecclesial and sacramental mediations that have derived from it.[3] The relevance of

---

[3] A similar reflection could be seen in Islamic developments, the new and different formulations of which presuppose the same monotheistic basis and certain Christian statements.

the picture I have here outlined would be even greater for Jewish monotheism if an analytic comparison were made with different religious approaches, such as those that have recently been propagated in the West by a certain eclectic orientalism. Here it is the drive toward a mystic fusion with the divinity, ever present and denied in all things, which predominates, a fusion and reconfusion attained by individual ecstatic techniques. I here only hint at such movements, disregarding the various assessments of them, in order to point out a number of distinctions and to underline their necessity.

Awareness of these distinctions and recognition of their present relevance goes hand in hand with knowledge of one's own origins, of the origins, that is, of one's culture, of the traditions – in this case the Jewish/Christian legacy – that have marked Western culture, even in its infinite variety and wanderings. Indeed there come moments in the history of recent European culture that may stand as illustrations of this movement towards a creative comparison with the past (I am thinking, above all, of the religious traditions that form a great part of this past). I refer, and these are important moments in my own sensibility and training, to two religious debates, one in the Russia of the early twentieth century, the other, of a more strictly historical-cultural and theological nature, in the Germany of the 1920s. But there are two examples on which I would particularly like to dwell as they are pertinent to the themes mentioned above (biblical monotheism, the prohibition of images), as well as to the issues the present essay will address (the apostasy of Mt. Sinai and the golden calf). I refer to two episodes of critical revision of the Jewish tradition, both occasioned by the external pressure of the Nazi threat.

The first case is that of Arnold Schönberg, who considers the history of the golden calf in his play *Moses and Aaron* (1932, unfinished). Here, the conflict between the purity of the monotheistic idea, represented by Moses and his silence, and the demands for religious expression that Aaron, with untiring eloquence, puts forward, takes center stage. The descent of Moses brings an abrupt end to the orgiastic explosion around the idol: "Holy is the generating force, holy is fertility, holy is desire!" (Act II, scene III). The contrast and incompatibility is total; there is no need even to refer to the complicated destruction described in the Bible (where the statue is smashed to pieces, burnt, disposed of). Here, the golden calf disappears and with it, at once, the crowd. But Moses' victory is only apparent – the community always needs forms of religious expression and Aaron, in his humanity and in his love for the people, is right not to yield. But more than that, is it not God himself who constantly supplies the people with his signs, his miracles, the column of fire and the cloud, the land that shall be given, the law? Yes, even the tablets are "an image, a part of thought." Moses himself suddenly glimpses the aporia and, in desperation, breaks the tablets. And on this note, on this indication of the desperate state of his soul, the work comes to a halt – a perfectly coherent conclusion, despite its formal incompletion – with Moses' cry: "Words, words, it is you I lack..." (Act II, scene V). Moses is inadequate, Aaron is inadequate, all words are inadequate, even those of Schönberg.

I will dwell at greater length on the second of the two cases, that of Sigmund Freud, because it stands at the origins of the present essay, at least as a distant suggestion. I refer, of course, to *Moses and Monotheism*, an apology of Judaism, even though it ruthlessly lays bare Judaism's supposed dependence on Egyptian monotheism and accuses it of a secret guilt, the reenactment of the primordial parricide, the killing of Moses.[4] Alone in his desperation, the Moses of Schönberg: alone in his tragic destiny, the "man-Moses" of Freud (although stoically composed in accepting his destiny – the disordered traits that Freud had already excluded in the Moses of Michelangelo are here attributed to later distortions. It is not on account of Moses' anger that the tablets are smashed, but because of the people's betrayal). And yet, after Moses' death, according to a process of the return of the repressed, Mosaic monotheism, through the work of the prophets, becomes a conscious and precious legacy of the people.

The entire conclusion of section C of the second chapter of the third essay, entitled "The Advance in Intellectuality," is worth reading:

> The Mosaic prohibition elevated God to a higher degree of intellectuality, and the way was opened to further alterations in the idea of God which we have still to describe. But we may first consider another effect of the prohibition. All such advances in intellectuality have as their consequence that the individual's self-esteem is increased, that he is made proud – so that he feels superior to other people who have remained under the spell of sensuality. Moses, as we know, conveyed to the Jews an exalted sense of being a chosen people. The dematerialization of God brought a fresh and valuable contribution to their secret treasure. The Jews retained their inclination to intellectual interests. The nation's political misfortune taught it to value at its true worth the one possession that remained to it – its literature. Immediately after the destruction of the Temple in Jerusalem by Titus, the Rabbi Jochanan ben Zakkai asked permission to open the first Torah school in Jabneh. From that time on, the Holy Writ and intellectual concern with it were what held the scattered people together.

---

[4]See Bori (1979).

> This much is generally known and accepted. All I have wanted to do is to add that this characteristic development of the Jewish nature was introduced by the Mosaic prohibition against worshipping God in a visible form.
>
> The pre-eminence given to intellectual labours throughout some two thousand years in the life of the Jewish people has, of course, had its effect. It has helped check the brutality and the tendency to violence which are apt to appear where the development of muscular strength is the popular ideal. Harmony in the cultivation of intellectual and physical activity, such as was achieved by the Greek people, was denied to the Jews. In this dichotomy their decision was at least in favour of the worthier alternative.[5]

Freud here defends the "spirituality" (*Geistigkeit, geistig*) of Israel when compared to other historical groups. Openly hostile to national socialist culture, whose ideal is physical development, Judaism is not hostile but necessarily extraneous to the Greek ideal of physio-psychic harmony; the *kalokagathia* precluded Jewish culture. With regard to Christianity, Freud is more reticent and postpones his judgment (he will say something at the end of *Moses*, section H). He does, however, clearly affirm the spiritual superiority of Israel, which he considers a result of the dematerialization (*Entmaterialisierung*) of the idea of God – itself a result of the prohibition to adore God in visible forms. Such spirituality consists essentially in the proud awareness that beyond any worldly political claim there is "something more," the values of the spirit which are contained in the Scriptures and in a devotion to them that gradually widens its arc to include every cultural calling.

As to Christianity, in the final pages one reads: "After the Christian doctrine had burst the framework of Judaism, it took up components from many other sources, renounced a number of characteristics of pure monotheism and adapted itself in many details to the rituals of the other Mediterranean peoples."[6] Here the judgment is implicit: even if sin and redemption achieve greater clarity in Christianity than in Judaism (and this, in a certain sense, is a sign of progress), in Christianity the transgression of the monotheistic commandment emerges once again with the formation of a religion of the son, a god who is no longer invisible. Judaism can still claim for itself the maximum fidelity to the originary law, and a superior

---

[5]S. Freud (1938) pp. 114-115. For this page of Freud's *Moses* was reserved the special destiny of being read by Anna Freud, standing in for her seriously ill father, at the International Congress of Psychoanalysis in Paris on August 2, 1938.

[6]Ibid., p. 136.

Introduction: In the Absence of Moses

spirituality both in its proper sense and probably, in Freud's intentions, also in the wider sense of spiritual values and of culture.

As I said earlier, these pages from *Moses* stand at the origins of this essay, at least as a distant suggestion. To my sensibility as a historian of the Christian tradition it immediately appears evident that the entire history of the relations (and non-relations) between Judaism and Christianity has been marked by the claim for greater spirituality advanced by the latter over the former, up until the precocious formation of the stereotypical opposition between flesh and spirit as essential categories of the anti-Jewish controversy. We can trace the formation of these categories applied to the conflict between Church and Synagogue through the anti-Jewish literature, using as a key the history of the interpretation of the biblical event narrated in Exod. 32.[7] This is a thread that will permit us to follow the long line of theological traditions and bring attention to the small variations, clues to the transformations (often deteriorations) in the Church/Synagogue relationship. Or better, it allows us to trace the self-consciousness of the Church compared to a Judaism denied or ignored.

Above all, I am interested in the establishment of the fundamental theses relative to Jewish idolatry formulated between the 2nd and 3rd centuries, and which view carnality as a characteristic peculiar to Judaism. Of course, the choice of a biblical motif has also made it necessary to consider the exegetic literature (commentaries, sermons etc.) relevant to the Exodus passage (and in the end this material has had the upper hand on the specifically anti-Jewish writings). So chapter one studies the debate on the "original sin" of the people and of Aaron in particular. It traces the admissions and apologies on the Jewish side, the exploitation of the fall on the Christian. Chapter two provides the core of the essay. It argues for the formation of a stereotype of Jewish carnality and the image of the servile people both

---

[7]There exists an imposing wealth of anti-Jewish literary material. Even accounting for recent contributions, it remains radically under exploited. The most complete body of work remains, as is well-known, that of Williams (1935). Concerning the high medieval latin aspects, the works of Blumenkrantz (1960 and 1963) are important. For a more recent period, see Moore (1921). After the two important works by Blumenkrantz (1946) and Simon (1948), more recent contributions of varying value have been made by Judant (1969), Hruby (1971) – which draws on Judant – Wilken (1971), Grego (1973), Efroymson (1975), De Lange (1976), Aziza (1977), Gelsi (1978), Poinsotte (1979), and recently and very usefully, Conzelmann (1981) and Schreckenberg (1982). Among the better recent editions of texts, I take the opportunity of noting in particular those dedicated to Sergius Stylites (*The Disputation against a Jew*, edited by A.P. Hayman, Lovanio 1973, CSCO 338) and to Jacob of Sarug (*Homelies contre les juifs*, edited by M. Albert, Turnhout 1976, PO 38).

as a necessary pole for Christian self-consciousness and as a means of affirming Christianity's own diversity and superiority. Finally, chapter three touches on the problems of the moral utilizations of the episode. Above all, it treats the crucial question of the transformation of the concept of idolatry. In order to allow those scholars who would like to devote further study to the biblical crux of the polemic, I have added two appendices. Appendix I covers the more strictly exegetical ground, considering the golden calf in the biblical tradition : (1) Old and (2) New Testament; (3) Ancient biblical versions; (4) the Koran. These are avowedly synthetic pages which aim only at supplying preliminary information, beginning with the specialized literature and exemplifying from the most practical and well-known sources. A second appendix deals with the (possible) relationship between golden calf and the old pagan accusation of onolatry (the adoration of an ass).

Non-specialist readers may, perhaps, be shocked by the incisiveness of my conclusions to this necessarily compact and analytic essay. In point of fact, they are such an integral part of the analysis, having come to light with it, that they seem to me at times almost superfluous. But that is not to say, excessive. In these matters, of which we speak so rarely, it is necessary to exceed a little in order to find their truth. For "after all, we are dealing with the truth, not with Christianity."[8]

---

[8]Troeltsch (1903) p. 446. I am also thinking of Coleridge, cited by Tolstoy in his answer to the condemnation of the Holy Synod of the Orthodox Russian Church (1901): "Whoever begins to love Christianity more than the truth, will love his sect or his Church more than Christianity and will finish by loving himself more than any other thing." See Bori and Bettiolo (1978) pp. 106 and 112 ff.

1

The Original Sin of the People

1. Terms

"The nearest Jewish equivalent to the concept of original sin." Thus has the idolatrous fall at the foot of Mt. Sinai – the first in the history of Israel – been described in post-biblical Jewish literature.[1]

Before going on to document this statement, I would like to reflect for a moment on the terms that are here brought into question, idolatry, sin, and original sin. Jewish monotheism is evidently incompatible with the cult of any divinity other than the God who reveals himself to Moses, and who we find in the history of the patriarchs. But it is also incompatible with any representation of the revealed God. This is the most urgent meaning of the condemnation of idolatry, the cult of images, whatever they may represent, be it even God himself. In fact, it has been argued that this is the capital lesson taught by the event narrated in chapters 32-34 of Exodus. Here, the people, through Aaron, do not give themselves other gods, but make for themselves an image of the Mosaic God, the God of the exodus. The text reads: "Here is your God, Israel, he who brought you out of the land of Egypt." Whatever the historical evolution that has led to the elaboration and reciprocal integration of the two incompatibles I mentioned above – the absolutism of monotheism and the obligation not to create images of the divinity – the two prohibitions are inseparable aspects of biblical monotheism. Regardless of the contradictions concerning this position present in biblical history, the position itself remains of enormous import. It characterizes and judges all further developments in

---

[1] Smolar and Aberbach (1968) p. 6. I have here availed myself greatly of this work, as well as of Ginzberg's *Legends*, vol. 3, pp. 119-24, for the following pages of my argument.

monotheism, which stand and fall according to whether or not the originary confession is maintained. From this standpoint, it becomes clear that idolatry – associating other gods with God, creating an image of God – is *the* sin par excellence: once this sin is committed the cardinal commandment is jettisoned and with it the whole covenant.

These have long been taxing thoughts, on which it was (and still is) difficult to hold full attention without being side-tracked. It is easier to consider them as already acquired knowledge and, without noticing perhaps, leave open vast spaces to incoherency. Biblical tradition, in this regard, focuses above all on two ultimately inseparable points. Idolatry comprises surrender to instinctual pressure, yielding to immediate needs, to *epithymia-concupiscentia*. Here, in the episode of the golden calf, that pressure is manifested in the people's need for a guide as they stand, consumed by panic, contemplating the immense space before them, with neither possibility of return nor visible goals. Elsewhere, instinctual pressure precipitates the people's need of reassurance before the most disturbing of experiences, such as sexual practice. It requires the comfort of a presiding *baal*, one of their own number, one who resembles them – someone who leaves neither man nor woman alone before something terrible, like death itself, which it resembles. On the other hand, the biblical and above all the sapiential tradition goes out of its way to denounce the intellectual perversion of idolatry, the shameful exchange of the glory of God, the glory of the people, for the appearance of an object anchored within the horizon of the things man can touch and manipulate. The traditions foreground the paradox (and the humiliation) in the people's belief that they are led, for example, by a sacred sign, while all the time it is they who created it and who carry it on their shoulders.

So the Jewish tradition looks on its history in a realistic light as the history of idolatrous falls and recoveries from those falls, as well as of deepening insights into the monotheistic legacy. The golden calf episode is therefore extremely significant. With no apologetic false veils, the memory of the fall is transmitted and the divine answer highlighted. This answer lies in the pedagogy of the law, the merciful gift which, from without, protects the people from the threats of assimilation, and from within channels but never suppresses instinctual energies, putting them under the yoke of obedience. With the cultual decalogue of Exodus 34 and all the expansions, there must no longer be any act which escapes the monotheistic confession: the elders are charged with further tightening the constricting net of the law so that, disregarding any distinctions between sacred and profane, it embraces all aspects of existence. If transgression must occur, then the covenant contemplates the possibility of repentance and expiation.

The Original Sin of the People

The Christian theological universe is altogether different, at least from the experience of the resurrection of Jesus onwards (it can be argued that the historical itinerary of Jesus does not differ substantially from that of the Jewish prophets). In this context, let us once again turn to terms like monotheism, idolatry, law, sin and consider whether all, or almost all the implications of these terms can be traced back to Jewish presuppositions. In the Christian milieu the value of these terms changes; nothing remains the same. Christian monotheism soon becomes the confession of the Christ, become Lord (*Kyrios*) on resurrection. A face, a humanity, an icon of God are now available (although this does not necessarily admit images into the cult, all the same the consequences must be drawn). Thus the anti-idolatrous monotheistic confession takes on the form we find in I Cor. 8: "We know that no idol exists in the world and that there is only one God...for us there is only one God, the Father, from whom all things come and for whom we exist: and there is only one Lord Jesus Christ, through whom all things exist and we through him" (vv. 4-6).

Here, the entire life of the believer is addressed to communion, to participation in Christ. Faith, sacraments, ethics, mysticism all concentrate on one point, belonging to the Lord Jesus. The great doctrinal text of the Old Testament of course remains (covering creation, revelation, redemption, eschatology etc.), but the law is devalued, especially in the Hellenistic contexts where the Christian mission reaps its greatest successes. That is, the protective barriers of the law become less crucial. To defend oneself against idolatry it is now enough to know Christ, to know that idols do not exist. So except out of concern for the weakest, who do not yet fully understand, one can even legitimately eat immolated meats before the pagan divinities (this is the solution that Paul adumbrates in the already mentioned I Cor. 8-10).

In sum, the law is certainly necessary, at least in its major principles, like the decalogue, but it is not sufficient. Indeed, the law as such may even engender the possibility of sin in those who were ignorant of it – we all remember the powerful introspective analysis of the law-*epithymia* (*concupiscentia*)-sin-death sequence raised by Paul in Rom. 7. Here, it is the law which paradoxically engenders desire, sin and death, as Adam's story, infinitely reenacted and present in each of us, shows. The transposition of the category of communion from the relationship with Christ to that with Adam determines an unheard of insight into the notion of original sin (above all in later Augustinian references). It is an ontological mutation which derives from a sort of incorporation in Adam and in his sin, symmetrical and opposed to the incorporation in the new Adam, Jesus Christ. This stands in sharp contrast with Judaism, where sin appears as an evil inclination counterbalanced by a good inclination present in man, but where the sin of Adam, as the sin of humanity in general, or the original sin of idolatry, the first sin of the people, although full of dire consequences, does not indelibly mark either the nature of man nor that of the people.

2. The People

Faced with the first idolatrous sin of the people, which the Bible does not hesitate to recount, Jewish tradition takes a complex stance. Side by side with candid admissions that the worship of the golden calf has been the sin par excellence, from which Israel has never been completely absolved, we meet a vast apologetic and polemical literature which aims at freeing Israel from this heavy burden of guilt.[2]

First, let us consider the admissions of guilt. Ancient rabbinic traditions do not hesitate to ascribe to Israel full responsibility for the betrayal. They concern themselves only with its gravity, which they calculate according to the degree of its premeditation – eleven days after the gift of the Torah to Moses, according to Eli'ezer ben Jakob; twenty-one, according to Simeon ben Yohai; two according to Simeon ben Halafta; the same day, according to others (Yehudah ben Il'ai); at the very moment they received the law, when the people said: "We will put into practice and do all the Lord has said" (Exod. 24, 7), according to R. Meir.[3]

Further, according to later traditions serious crimes were committed on the occasion of the idolatrous betrayal. These went beyond fornication ("revelry"), beyond the killing of Hur, son of the sister of Moses; they include the massacre of the seventy elders, of whom the Bible will speak later in Num. (11:23-24).[4]

The gravity of the situation emerges not only from the considerations on the premeditation, but also from the admission of its consequences, that is: punishment by shameful diseases,[5] loss of the signs and sacerdotal privileges,[6] condemnation to wander in the

---

[2]Smolar and Aberbach (1968) pp. 101 ff.
[3]ExR 32, 7 (488-89); Smolar and Aberbach (1968) pp. 103 ff.
[4]LvR 8, 1 (123); Smolar and Aberbach (1968) p. 104; Ginzberg, Legends, vol. 3, p. 123.
[5]SifreNm 25,1; LvR 14, 34 (215) and 15, 1 (232); NmR 5, 12 (182); Smolar and Aberbach (1968) p. 104.
[6]Smolar and Aberbach (1968) p. 105, with various texts including Mech.Ex 19, 6 (ed. J.Z. Lauterbach 2, 205-06).

desert.⁷ The worship of the golden calf is considered the worst sin committed by Israel and the forerunner of all other calamities.⁸ Indeed, since the biblical text itself speaks of a punishment for the sin on the day of the divine visit (Exod. 32:4), every calamity can be traced back to it: "There is no retribution in the world [for a Jew] which does not contain a small fraction [of the sin] of the first calf."⁹ A historical consequence of this first crime is not only exile, the loss of the spirit, but also the angel of death's seizing of power over Israel.

On the other hand, as I mentioned above, attempts are made to reduce the gravity of the fact. An early expression of the desire to attenuate the event is found in the marginal comment "one reads, one does not translate," which appears in an important targum (paraphrastic aramaic translation) to the Pentateuchs, the so-called Codex Neophyti. And the Mishnah authorizes the translation of the first part, but not the end of the biblical story (Exod. 32:21-25;35).

There are plenty of other clues that indicate how concerned the learned Jews were to avoid any contact between worship of the calf and other episodes, or biblical figures. Consider the stance adopted by Flavius Josephus and by Philo. While the latter is characterized by his concern to excuse Aaron and to moralise on the event,¹⁰ the former, Josephus, even though he describes the anxiety which seizes the Jews during the prolonged absence of Moses, and their joy at his return, completely omits the worship of the calf and the breaking of the first tablets.¹¹ There is, here, a concern to avoid furnishing pagan anti-semitism, which accused the Jews of worshipping an ass, with further ammunition.¹² But Josephus also wants to spare his readers embarrassment over a controversial event. So there is a desire to pass it over in silence wherever possible. (I shall deal later with the attempts to exculpate Aaron – attempts shared in this case by the Christian exegetic tradition.)

Similarly, rabbinic Judaism aimed to spare the people responsibility. To this end, it adopted various strategies. For instance,

---

⁷For example, ExR 21, 1 (354).
⁸Shab 17 a; Smolar and Aberbach (1968) p. 106.
⁹Smolar and Aberbach (1968) p. 106; Ginzberg, Legends, vol. 3, p. 120. See in particular ExR 32, 11 (496).
¹⁰De vita Mosis II 161-73, 270-74 (OEuvres 22, pp. 262-69, 312-15).
¹¹Ant. III 95-101 (Thackeray, pp. 360-65).
¹²See, for example, Tacitus, Hist. V 3: "Effigem animalis, quo monstrante errorem sitimque depulerant, penetrali sacravere." According to Tacitus, the Jews worshipped an ass in the Temple because Moses had followed a herd of asses in order to find water in the desert. See Gager (1972) pp. 127 ff. and Appendix II.

and most importantly, it foregrounds the undeniable fact (from the point of view of biblical testimony) that the history of the people is not brought to a halt with the fall at the foot of Mt. Sinai. God replaces the first tablets; the divine gifts are not withdrawn. Further, by way of excuse, the role of Satan and his followers is stressed.[13] And it is pointed out that the idolatrous event takes place before the covenant between God and the people has been perfected; Israel has not yet fully taken on its commitments, and so its responsibilities are less burdensome.[14]

Conversely, and still in Israel's support, attempts are made to outline God's own responsibilities. For instance, it was God who led Israel into temptation, detaining Moses for an overly long period. Moreover, his foresight could have avoided the fall. From this perspective, the very honour of God is at stake (this is a development of the arguments Moses uses when he intervenes on behalf of the people).[15] And in our last example, God's cosmos yields room to subtly equivocate over man's responsibility: if, in the vision of Ezekiel, one of the forms, alongside the lion, man and eagle, is that of a bull, then surely the worship of the calf is only a partial transgression?[16]

The Christian position (as can be glimpsed in Stephen's speech, Acts 7), takes different, even contradictory premises. Whereas Judaism admits guilt but at the same time proposes at least partial redemption, stressing the fact that pardon followed the crime and offering a series of apologetic expedients, the Christian polemic takes over the facts, exploits them, and attributes to the episode all the gravity of a first, fatal fall from which Israel would never recover. This argument appears from early Christian theology onwards. For instance, the author of Barnabas' Letter (first half of the second century) invites his readers to reflect:

> I ask you, furthermore, as one of you, who loves you one by one and all more than myself, to be on your guard and not to resemble certain people by accumulating your sins and saying our covenant is also theirs. It is ours, certainly: they, though, had already lost it as Moses received it. Scripture says: "Moses fasted on the mountain for forty days and forty nights, and received from the Lord the covenant, the stone tablets written by the finger of the hand of the Lord." But

---

[13] See also Smolar and Aberbach (1968), who, among other texts, avail themselves of ExR 32, 1 (477) and Shab 89-90. See also Ginzberg, *Legends*, vol. 3, pp. 120 ff.
[14] For example ExR 32,11 (495).
[15] For example, ibid. (500-06); see Smolar and Aberbach (1968) pp. 114 ff.
[16] There exist a number of versions of this line of reasoning: see Ginzberg, *Legends*, vol. 3, p. 122.

The Original Sin of the People

because they had turned to the idol they lost it. The Lord says: "Moses, Moses, go down at once for your people, those you brought out of Egypt, have sinned." Moses understood and threw away the two tablets he held in his hands: and their covenant was broken, until the covenant with Jesus, the beloved, was sealed in our hearts in the hope of faith in him.[17]

According to this version, it would appear that Moses did not even come down from the mountain and that the original divine intention was fulfilled: "Let my anger be vent against them and destroy them." No mention here of Moses' intercession, of the divine pardon, of the renewal of the covenant, the *deuterosis*.

Toward the end of the second century, Tertullian expresses a more nuanced version of the same line of thought. At the beginning of his *Against the Jews*, he explains Paul's remark "the elder will serve the younger" (Rom. 9:12; Gen. 25:23). To Tertullian, Esau stands for Israel, Jacob for the church. The most ancient people mirror Esau, serving the younger church because, having "abandoned God, [they] became slaves of the idols and, having left all that is divine, [they] abandoned themselves to the cult of the statues of the gods, when the people said to Aaron: 'Make us *elohim* to walk before us.'" Recalling other falls, and returning to Scripture, Tertullian concludes: "These facts show that they were always deemed guilty of the sin of idolatry."[18] The golden calf episode represents the "first steps of transgression."[19]

Speaking of this fact as the first retreat from God of the "unfaithful and ungrateful people,"[20] Cyprian locates Exod. 32 at the forefront of the anti-Jewish dossier with which he opens his collection of scriptural texts.[21] And as early as the middle of the second century, Justin underlines how it was only after the idolatry that God agreed to

---

[17]Ep. Barn. 4, 6-8. According to the Pseudo-Barnabas, this is traditional doctrine. He writes: "to those who love in order that nothing be ignored of what we have received" (4, 9). See Wengst (1971) p. 14. A parallel passage is in 14, 1-5: "We see and we look to see if the covenant, which he swore to our fathers he would give to the people, would really be given. He gave it, but they for their sins were not worthy of receiving it...[here he cites Exod. 32] Moses then received it, but they were not worthy of it. You will learn instead that it was us who received it." According to Prigent (1961) pp. 60 ff, the first text (4, 7-8) is secondary to the second (14, 1-3).
[18]Adv. iud. 1,6-7 (CC 2, 1340).
[19]Scorp. 3, 4 (CC 2, 1075): "primordia transgressionis"; see also Adv. Marc. IV 31, 3-4 (CC 1,630): "declinaverant vocationem tunc, primo dicentes ad Aaron..."; Adv. iud. 3,13 (CC 2, 1347): "et ideo, qui non populus dei retro, facti sumus populus eius."
[20]Bon. pat. 19 (CC 3 A, 129).
[21]Test. 1, 1 (CC 3, 6).

"accomodate himself" to the "unjust and ungrateful" people, to allow the making of sacrifices and the prescription of the sabbath – dispositions which were superfluous for the previous generations of the righteous.[22] Finally, a few decades later, polemicizing in his *Against Celsus* (the major apologetic text of ancient Christianity), and recalling the story of the golden calf, Origen assigns to a Jew the original lack of belief (*apistia*) of the people:

> And consider if it was not typical of this people (*kata tous autous*) despite all the miracles and manifestations, to be already disbelievers throughout the period in the desert, as is written in the law of the Jews: then, at the time of the extraordinary coming of Jesus, not to be convinced by the words he spoke with authority and by his miraculous actions carried out in full sight of the people. I think this allows those who so wish to establish that the disbelief of the Jews is consonant (*akolouthos*) with what is said of the people since their origins.

In fact, Origen explains, as it is the "habit" (*kata to ethos*) of the people to despise miracles, from the smallest to the largest, there is nothing strange in their "showing themselves twice to be disbelievers, at the beginning both of the ancient and the new covenants."[23] (Of course, Irenaeus has something to say in this context, but I will defer comment on his opinion.)[24]

In the fourth and fifth century – and in the most violent and definitive clash between Judaism and Christianity as theologies and cultures – the charge broadens. On the one hand, a retrospective link is established with Adam's sin: "Adam dies after eating and Israel after the manna."[25] On the other hand, and above all, a prospective link appears between the blasphemous gesture of idol worship and the crucifixion of the Son of God . "The king was derided in the desert and similarly the son of the king in Jerusalem. The father was exchanged for the calf and various idols, and the son for a blood-stained robber."[26] Indeed, I believe that the term *Horeb* (which is equivalent in another tradition to Sinai) permits commentators from Cassiodorus on to establish a link between the idolatrous episode and Calvary. Consider the following:

> Horeb means "Calvary," where we know that the Lord was afterwards killed in the flesh on the gallows of the cross: likewise, in a place of the same name, even then, in the desert of Horeb, those

---

[22]Dial. 19, 5-6 (Archambault, p. 88).
[23]C. Cels. II 74-75 (SC 132, 460).
[24]See chapter 2, section 3.
[25]John Chrysostom, Hom. I de tent. Dom.15 (PO 13, 124; see PG 57, 210; 61, 685).
[26]Ephraem, Serm. 3, 421 (CSCO 135, 84).

whose future progeny crucified Christ the Lord on Calvary, violated the divine cult with evil presumption.[27]

And the passage continues with speculation that gives systematic form to the above affirmations by compiling lists of Israel's sins in which the *reatus vituli* is the prototype of all idolatry,[28] *idolatriae caput*.[29] But I find the most striking expression of this link between capital sins in the work of a late doctor of the church, John of Damascus. In his sermon *In sanctum Parasceven* (Easter always reinvigorates anti-Jewish invectives), he aligns the "sodomitic cry" "go on, go on, crucify him" with the denial, the "atheism," he even says, which comes after Egypt. Both cases constitute a denial of the king. He writes: "You have denied your king: you will remain from now on without a king and will carry for eternity the yoke of slavery."[30]

3. Aaron

If Christian tradition is unanimous and ready to draw grave repercussions from the transgression, it moves more delicately when dealing with Aaron. Aaron cannot be dragged entirely into responsibility for the idolatry without contradicting the biblical event

---

[27]Exp. Ps. 105, 19 (CC 98, 964): "Horeb vero interpretatur Calvaria, ubi postea Dominum crucis patibulum carne constat occisum: ut ipso eodemque nomine iam tunc et in illo deserto Horeb culturam Domini nefanda praesumptione violarent, quorum posteritas erat in Calvariae loco crucifixura Dominum Christum." This is taken up by Rabanus Maurus, De univ. 7 (PL 111, 210); Bruno of Wurzberg, Exp. Ps. 105, 20 (PL 142, 386); Peter Lombard, Comm. Ps. 105, 19 (PL 191, 964). For the same scorn and criminal malice against Christ as had been manifested previously against Moses, see Rupert of Deutz, In. Os. III (PL 168, 18). This topic also appears in Peter Alfonsi, Dial. 2 (PL 157, 574): the crucifixion is a worse crime than the one committed in the desert. In truth, it is the Jew Moses, Peter's mediator, who speaks and admits the gravity of the sin but who also underlines that divine mercy allowed Israel to survive.
[28]Rupert of Deutz, In. Os. I (PL 168, 44). See previously Cyril of Alexandria, In Am. III (Pusey, p. 474). Lists of idolatrous Acts: see for example Ephraem, Comm. ev. conc. XI 8 (SC 121, 199-200): Israel has a calf in the desert, two calves with Jeraboam, the four-faced idol of Manasse. Samuel Marochianus, Lib. Mess. event. praeter. 6 (PL 149, 342): four sins of the Jews: the *venditio* of Joseph, the golden calf, the killing of prophets and the *venditio iusti* par excellence, Jesus. See also Raymond Martini, Pugio fidei III 3, 16 (ed. Carpzov, Leipzig 1687, p. 845); see also II 1 (p. 261), on the sins of the people.
[29]Rupert of Deutz, De vict. verbi Dei V 2 (PL 169, 1317). It is for this sin that divine vengeance strikes the people, "quia repleti sunt olim" (the satisfaction of the idolatrous revelry): "propter haec quae peccaverunt, ex quo vitulum fecerunt, proiecisti eos nunc et indurasti cor eorum" (De s. Trin 27, In Isa. 19-10; CC cont. med. 23, 1471).
[30]In s. Parasc. 6 (PC 96, 596-718).

and the overall role he is assigned despite the fall. So even for the Christians, the aim is to save Aaron.

Jewish apologetics, more or less known and available, supplied useful precedents in this matter. For instance, Flavius Josephus, Philo and the author of *Antiquitates Biblicae* are ready to exculpate Aaron. Josephus and Philo accomplish this simply by omitting to mention him; the author of *Antiquitates Biblicae*, by contrast, offers significant and consistent defensive tracts on his behalf. First, Aaron attempts to encourage the people by inviting them to be patient, he is then seized by fear as he sees their presumption grow. Finally, the people themselves throw the gold into the fire whence (we are not told how) the calf takes form.[31]

In the later paraphrase in the Targum of Pseudo-Jonathan, Aaron sees Hur dead before him. He is overcome by fear and consequently yields to the request for an idol. But his painful cry "feast for the Lord tomorrow" foretells disaster for the people.[32] Aaron is similarly and variously exculpated in post-biblical Jewish literature. Consider the following characterizations: Aaron is frightened by a devil who tricks him into believing Moses is dead; Aaron must surrender before a tumult of the people led by philo-Egyptian elements, a tumult during which Hur dies – Aaron does not fear for his life, but the murder of the priest and prophet by Israel would add injustice to injustice and would not be received with mercy: in such circumstances, one is right to yield; Aaron plays for time by asking to build the altar himself; Aaron asks difficult questions, hoping that the women will not give up their ornaments (and, in fact, they do not, but the men have theirs and use them); Aaron lets the gold fall into the flames, while the rest is done by the fire, or by magic, or by the devil. Through these well-known

---

[31] See Ant. bibl. XII 2 (SC 229, 126): "Et dum esset in monte corruptum est cor populorum, 'et congregati sunt ad Aaron, dicentes: fac nobis deos,' quibus serviamus, quemadmodum habent et ceterae gentes, 'quoniam Moyses ille,' per quem facta sunt mirabilia coram nos, raptus est a nobis. 'Et dixit ad eos Aaron': Aequo animo estote. Moyses enim veniet, et appropiabit nobis iudicium, et legem illuminabit nobis, et superexcellentiam Dei exponet de ore suo, constituens iusticias generi nostro. Et haec loquente eo non obaudierunt ei, ut compleretur verbum quod dictum est in tempore quo peccavit populus aedificans turrim, cum dixit Deus: Et nunc nisi prohibeam eos, 'omne quod praeviderint sibi facere praesumunt' deterius [Gen. 11, 6]. Timens autem Aaron quoniam virtutificati erant populi valde, 'dixit ad eos: Afferte nobis inaures mulierum vestrarum.' Et petierunt viri unusquisque mulierem suam, et statim dederunt. Et miserunt eas in ignem, et effigiata sunt in figuram, et exivit vitulus conflatilis."

[32] See the translation of the relevent passage from the Targum in Appendix. I 3.

The Original Sin of the People

characterizations,[33] pity and imagination attempt to protect the sanctity of Aaron against the insults of biblical truth.

These same concerns are passed down to Christian interpreters, but not immediately. It appears that the figure of Aaron receives their attention only from the beginning of the fourth century. But from this moment onwards, the founder of the priesthood is protected by Christian exegesis through means that recall the Jewish apologetic inventions.

Consider the stance taken by Diodore of Tarsus (who died around 390), master to John Chrysostom and Theodore of Mopsuestia. Antiochian as to exegetic school and so attentive to the "letter," he passionately discusses the communion (*koinonia*) of Aaron along with the sin of the people. He denies that Aaron shares the responsibility; he shows him as he pleads with the people to elect another leader if they want to make *elohim*, tells of how he tried to stop the people with the difficult demand for the precious metals and, finally, of how when forced to make the calf, Aaron tried to prolong the operation until the return of Moses.[34]

Macarius the Great similarly vindicates Aaron. In one of the fifty sermons attributed to him, he underlines how Aaron was forced to order the collection of the gold which, when thrown into the fire, "turned into an idol as if the fire imitated [the people's] decision." That is, the supernatural act gave external form to the idolatrous choice which had already been made in the people's heart.[35] And towards the middle of the 5th century, Cyril of Alexandria affirms that Aaron's statement "these are your gods" is a kind of ironic warning aimed at jolting the memory, "the anamnesis of the things worked by God."[36] About a century later Procopius of Gaza attributes the same desperate pedagogical intention to Aaron.[37]

But Ephraem offers the clearest witness of the passage to Christianity of Judaism's apologetic expedients. In his commentaries on Exodus, about the middle of the fourth century, he suggests that with Hur now dead, and fearing other crimes, or that the people will perhaps create more than one calf or return to Egypt, Aaron hopes in

---

[33] See Smolar and Aberbach (1968) pp. 109-11; Ginzberg, *Legends*, vol. 3, pp. 121-23.
[34] The passage remains extant only as a fragment. See Deconinck (1912) p. 146. For an identical point of view in Theodoretus of Cyrrhus see Interr. 66 (PG 80, 292).
[35] Hom. 11, 2 (Dorries, Klosterman and Kroeger, p. 97).
[36] Glaph. Exod. III (PG 69, 528-29).
[37] Comm. Exod., *ad loc.* (PG 87, 663-64).

vain that the request for the women's gold will prevent the consummation of the intention to create gods. It is only when driven by fear (the Syriac version, the Peshitta, keeps Exod. 32:5: "Aaron was afraid") that Aaron finally is forced into making the sacrifice.[38] Even a spurious text attributed to John Chrysostom similarly describes the creation of the idol and exonerates Aaron as much as possible. It reads: "Take your gold coins, throw them into the fire and if something come of it, that will be your god. And an animal with a bovine head came out."[39]

The latin tradition is more restrained, at least as far as the reception of Jewish traditions is concerned. But although hesitant in apportioning responsibility for idolatry ("we can neither excuse such a great priest, nor dare we condemn him"), Ambrose does assert that Aaron asked *coactus* the people for their ornaments.[40] Augustine is of the same opinion: according to him, Aaron "did not consent induced, but yielded constrained."[41] Further, he suggests that by giving the order to melt the ear rings and demanding arduous, even impossible tasks Aaron hoped to distract the people from their idolatrous intentions.[42] This argument has had some success. From Augustine it was passed on, for example, to Rupert of Deutz,[43] to the interlinear and ordinary gloss and to other later authors.[44]

Medieval exegesis can draw more openly on the Jewish tradition. Indeed, Peter Comestor, Nicholas of Lyra, Dionysius the Carthusian (between the middle of the twelfth and fifteenth centuries) all refer directly to it. In Comestor, the tragic death of Hur, the request made to the women, the magic-demonic fusion of the idol – "tradunt hebraei" –

---

[38]Comm. Exod., *ad loc.* (CSCO 153,131-32). The same story of Hur is in Comment on Exodus by Iso'dad of Merv (17,12; CSCO 179, 48-49), where the unsuccessful attempt to stop the making of the calf by putting pressure on the women's love of their ornaments appears. Finally, Aaron throws the precious stones into the fire saying: "Lord, do according to your will" (30, 1-4, p. 73).
[39]C. iud. (PG 48, 1079).
[40]Ep. 66,3 (PL 16, 1278).
[41]Civ. Dei XIV 11 (CC 48, 433).
[42]See Quaest. Exod. 141 (CC 33, 135): "Quod iubet Aaron inaures demi de auribus uxorum atque filiarum, unde illis facerent deos, non absurde intelligitur difficilia praecipere voluisse, ut hoc modo eos ab illa intentione revocaret; factum tamen illud ipsum difficile, ut esset aurum ad faciendum idolum, propter eos notandum putavi, qui contristantur, si quid tale propter vitam aeternam divinitus fieri vel aequo animo tolerari iubeantur."
[43]In Exod. IV 16 (PL 168, 221-22).
[44]Gloss. ord. (PL 113, 287); but see also Calvin: "rem odiosam ... exigit" (Comm. lat. on Exod., *ad loc.;* Opera 25, Corp. ref. 53, 82).

all appear.⁴⁵ And these elements, along with others, are present in the work of the other two authors. However they are not all viewed sympathetically. For example, although Nicholas of Lyra finds in Rabbi Solomon ben Yitzaq (the Jewish exegete of the eleventh century known as Rashi) the presence of Egyptians or philo-Egyptians among the Jews of the exodus, the misunderstanding over the end of the 40 days and Moses' tardiness, the satanic fiction of Moses' death, the death of Hur and the demand for the jewels, the magically animated calf, Aaron's attempt to delay the idolatrous cult by making the altar himself, Nicholas himself does not hold with many of these suggestions. Indeed, he grasps their general apologetic intent in favour of the entire people and does not let it pass. He comments, "The great wish to yield to idolatry is clear."⁴⁶ Similarly, Dionysius the Carthusian accepts various traditional considerations ("the high priest made taxing demands on the women"), but rejects others such as the story of Hur (why did Scripture not give the news?). Thus, while admitting that Aaron was induced by external pressure and fear of worse crimes, he refuses the magic/satanic creation of the calf. He writes: "The Scripture of both Testaments ascribes it as much to Aaron as to the people."⁴⁷ The critique of the legendary elements which underlies biblical clarity is here beginning to take form, and opens the way for the net Lutheran condemnation: "Aaron is here at his worst."

But the Lutheran clarification is not without precedents in the Christian reflection, even if the New Testament versions do not involve Aaron directly in the charge. In a generally homiletical context, the Christian authors underline, at times with almost reformist tones, that where sin abounds, including that of the *archiereus*, of the high priest, there also abounds mercy. Consider the following three quotations:

> And even if the the whole people sinned, divine philanthropy was not defeated. The people made the calf and God did not abandon philanthropy: men denied God, but God did not deny himself....Yet, it was not only the people who sinned but also Aaron, the high priest.⁴⁸
>
> Aaron, anointed and ordained first priest, gratified by the gift of the Holy Spirit, yielded to the impious requests of the iniquitous people, erected the image of the calf and offered sacrifices with other Levites: and yet he received mercy.⁴⁹

---

⁴⁵Peter Comestor, Hist. schol.: Lib. Exod. 73 (PL 198, 1189-90): "De his omnibus quae dicta sunt de vitulo, tacet Iosephus," and refers to Jewish traditions: "excusant se hebraei," "tradunt quidam," "tradunt hebraei."
⁴⁶Nicholas of Lyra, Post. tot. Bibl. I (Strasburg 1592) *ad loc.*
⁴⁷En. Exod., *ad loc.* (Opera 2, p. 100).
⁴⁸Theodoret of Cyrrhus, Haer. fabul. comp. V 28 (PG 83, 549).
⁴⁹Theodoret of Cyrrhus of Ciro, Haer. fabul. comp. V 28 (PG 83, 549).

Neither Moses nor Aaron, neither David nor Peter, first of the apostles, nor Paul risen to the third heaven can claim they are free of sin. So I also try to save myself only with faith: "with faith," I say, not with my works, until the Philanthropist will also say to me: "Your faith has saved you, go in peace."[50]

Similar tones are evinced in latin and western milieux,[51] above all when Aaron is seen as the prototype of the shepherd who fails in the mission given him by an immediate superior[52] and when he is contrasted to Mary and Martha – Moses up on the mountain, and Aaron down below "implicated in the world."[53] Aaron, then, is an embarrassing and complex figure. Gregory of Nissa already glimpses this truth when he denounces the ambiguity (*homonymia*) that lurks beneath the name "brother":

> Scripture has clearly shown us the equivocal nature of the name brother: not always does the same term mean the same thing, the same name can be understood as meaning contradictory concepts. One thing is the brother who removes the Egyptian tyrant, another altogether the brother who makes the idol for the Israelites, even if they do have the same name.[54]

For Gregory, we are here dealing with theoria, a general anthropological reflection. But the singling out of this duality (one joining with other dualities which, as is well known, mark the history of the exodus) grasps a precise human truth (also perhaps a historical truth in Gregory's own experience) that the apologetic concerns tended to gloss over.

4. Supernatural Interventions

In the background, theological imagination introduces supernatural and demonic agents not only to tinge the scene with more dramatically complex colours, but also to return the episode to the irreducible ground

---

[50] Anastasius Sinaita, Or. Ps. 6 (PG 89, 1128). Areta of Cesarea is right to note that Aaron's sin is not attenuated by the people's unanimity (symphony): see Scripta minora 14 (ed. Westering, Lipsia 1968, p. 163). For the same theme of sin and pardon among Byzantine writers see Michael Glycas, Ann. II 157 (PG 158, 304); among the Syrians see Martyrius (Sahdona), Ep. 4, 117 (CSCO 255, 52).
[51] See for example the pseudo-Augustine, Lib. quaest. 8,1 (CSEL 50, 32): "et ipse peccaverat," and so could not see the uncovered face of Moses. See also Facundus, Pro def. trium capit. XII 3 (PL 67, 832).
[52] Among monastic rules see PL 103, 552. See also Bruno of Segni, Exp. Exod., ad loc. (PL 164, 367): "Multum peccant et illi sacerdotes ... si delinquenti populo favent et eorum stultitiam non redarguunt."
[53] See Peter Damian, De contemp. saec. 27 (PL 145, 280).
[54] De vita Mosis II 210 (SC 1bis, 99).

The Original Sin of the People

of the biblical situation – a story that takes place, when all is said and done, between God and the Adversary; man has only a secondary role.

We have seen how Satan is introduced into the story of the calf by Jewish apologetics, for which he has the effect of attenuating responsibility. It is he, according to Targum Pseudo-Jonathan, who perverts the heart of the Jews by inciting them to hubristic practices;[55] the philo-Egyptians and in particular, the two magicians who mould the idol, are his emissaries,[56] and their deception is all the more convincing because the calf appears to be alive and even emits lowing sounds.[57]

The Koran also seems to bear on these and other traditions of more problematic identification. It reads: "The men of Moses made for themselves a calf with their ornaments, a body which emitted lowing sounds" (sura 7:148). But later on (sura 20:85-97), there appears the mysterious figure of the Samaritan, gifted with magic powers of uncertain origins and who, throwing into the fire "a fist of earth from the saint's foot (Gabriel? Moses?) causes the appearance of a calf, a body which emitted lowing sounds."[58]

The satanic presence is noted more openly in the Christian tradition. But if it appears early in the *Acta Thomae* (it was the demon who deceived the crowd in the desert when they made the calf),[59] only later, and in the context of more general speculations, is it found in greater authors. Thus Gregory the Great attributes the fall of the Jews to greed: In it, he sees the work of the devil as he creeps over the belly.[60] And medieval authors find in the calf the devil himself ("they took into their midst the devil and served him").[61] Indeed, in a symmetrical relation with the image of the body of Christ, and nourished by Augustinian suggestions, they elaborate the metaphor of a *corpus diaboli*, the "society of pagans devoted to idols." It becomes an easy next step to see in the destruction of the golden calf the destruction

---

[55]See later, App. I.3.
[56]See Ginzberg, *Legends*, vol. 3, pp. 129 ff.
[57]Pirqe de Rabbi Eleazer, ed. G.Friedlander 45 (355). A tradition known to Dionysus the Carthusian and Nicholas of Lyra.
[58]See later, App.I.4.
[59]Acta Thomae 32 (Lipsius and Bonnet, vol. 2, t. 2, p. 149).
[60]Reg. past. III 19 (PL 77, 81).
[61]Rabanus Maurus, Alleg. s. Scr., "vitulus" (PL 112, 1082). See also Rupert of Deutz, De vict. verbi Dei V 2 (PL 169, 1319): "Vitulus ille, immo in vitulo diabolus."

and conversion of gentile society.[62] Pierre of Poitiers, for example, explains: "the calf is the body of the devil, the Church of the idolatrous who, having removed the image of God, take on the image of the devil."[63]

Even more fascinating, but useless for our concerns, which hinge on the responsibility for the historical event, is the observation made by a German theologian of the 12th century, Gerhoh of Reichersberg. In line with the complex of all those who are radically tied to the literal, to the law, he sees the *corpus diaboli* in the golden calf – once the tablets are broken and the spiritual sense has emerged, through teaching, the demonic body, the letter, goes to pieces.[64]

In sum, in the Christian tradition the importance given to supernatural agents is modest when the facts are considered. This is hardly surprising because here there is no need to exonerate the people (a need that existed neither in Stephen's invective nor in Paul's parenesis). On the contrary, it is incumbent on Christians to individuate in the golden calf and fix in it, to the point of stereotypical repetition (lists of sins), a capital episode in the history of the Jewish people, which Christians see as a history of ingratitude and falls.

---

[62] See Peter Damian, Serm. 6 (PL 144, 536). For expressions drawn from Augustine, C. Faust. 22, 92-93 (PL 42, 462-63); see also En. Ps. 61, 9 and 73, 15 (CC 39, 780,1015).

[63] Alleg. tab. Moysi 29vb (ed. Moore and Corbett, Notre Dame, Ind. 1938, p. 178).

[64] Comm.Ps. 105, 23 (PL 194, 655): "Tabulas fregit, et vitulum in frustra conscidit, quia lege per expositores fracta spiritualis sensus exsilit, qui corpus diaboli per praedicatores comminuit." For the link between practice and persistence in the law by the Jews after Christ and the Roman conquest, on the one hand, and the demonic influence, on the other, see Raymond Martini (Pugio fidei II 3, 9; Carpzov, p. 789). Referring to "Jewish traditions," he recalls the Talmud, Meil I, where however I have not found the text adopted by Martini and quoted more analytically ibid. p. 456: "Deus iudaeis per romanos abstulit sabbatum, et circumcisionem et alia caerimonia: 'confregit quippe in ira furoris sui omne cornu eorum' [Sal 75:2], de quibus unum erat lex ... et numquam restituit eis nec per se, neque per angelos neque per prophetam vel alium virum sanctum: sed ipsi iudaei recuperarunt circumcisionem, et sabbatum et caetera per diabolicum miraculum ... Nullus igitur ulterius, nisi sit penitus daemoniacus, observare debet ea quae Deus abstulit et diabolus tam liberaliter et libenter iudaeis visibiliter se ingerendo restituit. Quando enim vel ubi unquam scienter diabolus homini boni aliquid, nisi forte ubi prospexit malum maius et pessimum sibi ex eo imminere finaliter, procuravit? Cui unquam boni aliquid nisi fallendi studio pervasit? Nunquid ipse est, qui primos homines quasi utiliter eis consulendo fefellit? Nonne ipse contra sanctum Iob ipsum etiam Deum provocavit? An ignorant iudaei miseri, quod diabolus fuit, qui patres suos ad adorandum vitulum pertraxit?"

The Original Sin of the People

But in the Jewish reflection on the story, we find a different situation. Here, in part because Judaism necessarily lacks the elaboration of original sin present in its Christian counterpart, the event takes on grave consequences. As a result, for Judaism it becomes crucial to look for external extenuating circumstances (the immature condition of Israel, above all) to localize external factors and agents, behind which stands the devil. On the other hand, the Jewish response to the episode of the golden calf also calls God himself into question. There emerges the contradiction of God saving and tempting, protecting and putting to the test. Indeed we find the following comment: "God has not freed *us* from Egypt, but only himself, he being their prisoner."[65] But this objection, expressed in the murmurs of the people, might not be so blasphemous as first appears given that Moses, in his prayer of intercession, reminds God how and in what way his honor is at stake. He prays: "Why let the Egyptians say: 'He brought them out in a malicious manner, to have them perish in the mountains and disappear from the earth?'" (Exod. 32:12).

Let us now pull our two traditions, Jewish and Christian, together. The Christian tradition differs drastically from the Jewish. It shifts the focus for the problem, if at all, only onto Adam's sin, the *felix culpa*. It achieves its greatest insights when, ignoring the reiterated manifestations of divine pardon, it links (with Augustine) Horeb and Calvary and draws out the similarities between the two crimes, idolatry and crucifixion, establishing two series of crimes regularly perpetrated by the people, idolatry and the murder of prophets. This, the murder of prophets, is the second and major theme of the anti-Jewish polemic.[66] But the shared root of the polemic's two themes is unearthed when we move from external action to origins, to the fundamental thrust that, first in the prophets, later in the Christian polemic, underlies both the idolatrous behaviour and the murderous deicide, that is, Jewish "carnality."

---

[65]Ginzberg, *Legends*, vol. 3, p. 123.
[66]There has been no systematic enquiry into this theme as concerns post-biblical Christian literature. The grounds for such a work have, however, been laid by Steck (1967).

2

Jewish Carnality

1. Terms

Job cries to God, freely venting his bitterness, "Do not condemn me! Tell me why you are my enemy ... Do you perhaps have eyes of flesh, do you see as mortal man sees?" (Job 10: 2.4). No, God does not have eyes of flesh; God is Spirit. This flesh/spirit polarity is not an opposition like sacred/profane, nor does it comprise two transcendent principles. Rather, it ultimately refers back in biblical tradition to the foundations of monotheism. Flesh is the creatural reality, born of God, made by Him – yet distinct from him, capable of opposing him and of confiding in itself even to the point of self-destruction. Spirit is God, other than the world, an intangible presence – yet creator and giver of life. Thus the prophets experience a Spirit, and that Spirit sends them out into the world to shake up a carnal people. We read in Jeremiah: "Cursed be the man who trusts in man, who places his trust in the flesh and whose heart is far from the Lord" (Jer. 17:5). Not even in the secessionist practice of the Qumran community is the prophetic request turned into a call to abandon the "flesh"; it always comprises a call to obey the law – which contains, supports and guides all actions toward the confession of the single God.

The flesh/spirit polarity plays an important role in Christian milieux, especially in Pauline writings (and, in a slightly different way, in John's). Let us take the resurrection as our starting-point. Here, death has destroyed the *sarx*, Jesus' mortal flesh, but God has resuscitated Christ through the power of the Spirit. It is certainly not Jesus' soul which appears to the disciples, rather they encounter his transfigured, glorious, spiritual body (*soma*, says Paul, never *sarx*). And it is with his body that the disciples are united. Indeed the sacramental act, baptism or eucharist, constitutes participation in

Christ's body (*soma*, but John speaks more paradoxically of *sarx*). Yet the entire ethic consists in ridding oneself of the flesh and being in Christ, following the Spirit. In fact, these major New Testament writings include hardly any trace of the Hellenistic body/soul dualism. Carnal or spiritual comprises the whole man, body and soul together, according to whether or not he joins in Christ through the Spirit. Thus, in the "spirituality"of Paul, in his struggle against "carnality," there is no residue of moralism – to live in the Spirit must have been an experience of liberation so giddying that in the interests of realism Paul had to restrain himself (thus revealing traces of his own personal discipline).

Within Christianity, this opposition soon serves to justify the distinction, the distance, the superiority of the Christian way over its Jewish counterpart. The Christ according to the flesh comes from the stock of David. What is crucial is his glorious body, risen through the power of the Spirit, which no longer belongs to Israel but to the believers, whatever their stock, whether or not they came from Israel according to the flesh. Christianity's opposition to the law thus becomes opposition between the letter (the materiality, the carnality of Scripture) and the Spirit: "The letter kills, the Spirit gives life" (2 Cor. 3:6).

Faithfulness to the land, loyalty to the people, participation in the cult in the Temple, are now supplanted by loyalty to a new reality, to a new personal lordship, the glorious *Kyrios*. Consequently, the critique of Jewish institutions becomes more radical. But the change is gradual – the first Christian community in Jerusalem, as is well-known, still frequents the Temple, and without falling into any perceptible contradiction it affirms its own identity within Israel by breaking bread in the houses. It is only with Stephen's speech (Acts 7) that Jewish institutions and the reality of the people become the object of a condemnation that remotely yet persistently strikes at the very roots of the people's infidelity and its resistance to the Christian innovation. Under the pressure of the demands made by his mission, Paul elaborates the antithesis between Israel according to the flesh and the "Israel of God" (Gal. 6:16), while in John a total split seems to be broached. On the one hand stand the Christians, children of God, not of flesh and blood; on the other stand the Jews, who have the devil for a father and are murderous from the outset (John 8:48).

2. Carnality

To build on these premises, the ancient Christian anti-Jewish polemic draws further documentation from Scripture. There, seeking out its remotest roots, it goes out of its way to associate the killing of prophets and of Christ (see also 1 Thess. 2:15) with its ultimate goal of locating a negative carnality in the Jews. It finds confirmation of its foundation stone, the opposition between the two Israels as an opposition between flesh and spirit. There is, then, an originary and stable core of resistance, of stubbornness, of deafness which in the eyes of the polemicists surrounds the matrix of Judaism's irreducible difference. For the polemicists, to attack this nucleus did not mean making efforts to penetrate its difference. Far from that: it meant attacking it with equal violence, often multiplying their accusations to the point of abuse.

My purpose here and now is not to put order into this literature of abuse by producing catalogues and lists.[1] Rather, I intend to discover from closer quarters what underlies the Christian approach and highlight the flesh/spirit duality and its subsequent degeneration by tracing the accusation of originary idolatry.

The biblical polemic against idolatry (this can be better gauged in the Appendix I) comprises two fundamental aspects. One, which is especially taken up by Paul, foregrounds idolatry's ethical dimension, its rebellion, disobedience, surrender to instinctual drives, to *epithymia*, established by 1 Cor. 10:6 as the general category containing all the successively listed sins. The other aspect highlights the intellectual distortion and the materialistic manipulation of the divinity present in idolatry. This concern appears in prophetic and sapiential reflection, as well as in Paul's indictment of pagan idolatry, which reads "While they claimed to be wise, they became foolish and exchanged the glory of the incorruptible God [Ps. 105:20 and therefore Exod. 32.] for the image and the figure of corruptible man, of birds, of four-legged beasts and reptiles." Immorality is the consequence, not the cause, of error: "For this reason, God abandoned them to their own impurity, which follows the desires of their heart" (Rom. 1:22). This aspect, as has been seen, returns in Stephen's speech (where, however, as in Ps. 105:13-14, nostalgia for Egypt is also apparent).

Interestingly, this second attitude is revived by the anti-Jewish polemic, but relatively late at the beginning of the fourth century.[2]

---

[1]This task has been accomplished by Juster (1914) vol. 1, pp. 44 ff.
[2]Origen's polemic differs when he warns against the dangers represented by worldly knowledge, figured as the Egyptian gold out of which the the calf is made: see Ep. Gregor. 3 (SC 148, 190-192). This theme recurs in Peter Damian who, basing himself on Rom. 1 and drawing on the remark concerning the gold used to make the calf, develops his characteristic anti-intellectualistic polemic: "Aureus autem vitulus fuisse describitur, quia videtur idolatria ritus velut a sapientibus institutus ... Aureus itaque fuit vitulus, quia mundi sapientes ante

Here, we find authors who congratulate themselves on having applied, by analogy, a more general theological reflection, pertinent to being itself and to the knowableness of God, to denounce the original idolatry of the Jews. Thus, for example, Athanasius of Alexandria reprimands the Pharisees for not recognizing the very clear signs offered by Jesus:

> It would have been the same for them to dare say, seeing the order of the cosmos and the providence that guides it, that even the creation came from Beelzebub: that even the sun rises obeying the devil and thanks to him the stars turn in the sky. If these are the work of God, so even those are the work of the Father, and if those are the work of Beelzebub, these necessarily must also be the work of Beelzebub. Where for them is "in the beginning God created the sky and the earth?" But their folly is not strange because the fathers of this opinion of theirs, in the desert, just after leaving Egypt, while making a calf and attributing to it the gifts which had come from God, said: "These are your Gods."[3]

This manoeuvre of recollecting the intellectual profile, the knowledge of God, to which one can have access (according to Paul's letter to the Romans), but which has been betrayed by the Jews who, through laxity and stupidity,[4] turned to those who are not gods (*kata physin*, according to nature), is characteristic of Cyril of Alexandria, a great enemy of the Jews.[5] The same reflection also appears in the writings of John of Damascus. There we read:

> They had as gods the same moulded objects and they adored them as gods, they who were the dwelling place of devils. And as they rendered homage to the creation and not to the creator, the divine apostle says [Rom. 1, 23]: "They who exchanged the glory of the incorruptible God for the image of corruptible man, and of birds, and of four-legged beasts and of reptiles, have rendered homage to the creature instead of to the creator."[6]

But while the intellectual definition of idolatry, which comes principally from the sapiential tradition, is found wherever exegesis and treatises of various kinds address the issue (in an increasingly abstract way as the memory of paganism fades), the line followed when dealing with the Jews is that suggested by Paul in 1 Cor. 10

---

novam gratiam fidei demoniacae culturae fuisse probantur auctores ... [here he cites Rom. 1: 21-23]. Per hanc itaque sapientiae vanitatem poetae, philosophi, magi, siderum rimatores omniumque disciplinarum liberalium instructi peritia, prodigiosa demoniorum solebant adorare figmenta" (Serm. 6; PL 144, 536).

[3] Ep. 4 a Serap. 16 (PG 26, 661 = CSCO 273, 7).
[4] De ador. Sp. et ver. I (PG 68, 144).
[5] In Na. 1, 2, 3 (Pusey, p. 5).
[6] C. imag. calumn. II 8; III 5 (ed. Kotter, Berlino, 1975, pp. 74 ff).

(which is *not* an anti-Jewish text). The idolatrous transgression is, then, for the above reason, described as a prevarication of instinct, of lust over the intellect. In it is seen clearly the carnal character of the Jewish people, their sensuality. Well in the foreground, as in Paul, and later in a long line of authors, appears the conclusion to the idolatrous scene: the people who "eat, drink and make revelry" (Exod. 32:6). It is their nostalgia for Egypt, their need to "sit down" which causes the idolatrous perversion.

This is by far the most common line of interpretation. However we should remember that the targumic tradition identified pride as the fundamental cause of idolatry and saw in Satan its final cause. Pride was suggested by Nehemiah, too.[7] And the Pseudo-Philo's *Antiquitates biblicae*, which sees in the fact of the golden calf the fulfillment of the prophecy dating back to the tower of Babel, clearly blames pride in the following: "They did not obey him so that the word, spoken at the time the people who built the tower sinned, was fulfilled, when God said: 'And now, if I don't prevent this, they will be ever more presumptuous and will do whatever they want.'" Yet, the suggestion that idolatry derives from pride proves completely secondary when we set it against the massive insistence on sensuality.[8]

Philo may be considered one of the originators of the line of interpretation that blames sensuality. He writes:

> When Moses had gone up into the mountain, and was there several days communing privately with God, the men of unstable nature, thinking his absence a suitable opportunity, rushed into impious practices unrestrainedly, as though authority had ceased to be, and forgetting the revenge they owed to the Self-Existent, became zealous devotees of Egyptian fables. Then, having fashioned a golden bull, in imitation of the animal held most sacred in that country, they offered sacrifices which were no sacrifices, set up choirs which were no choirs, sang hymns which were very funeral chants, and, filled with strong drink, were overcome by the twofold intoxication of wine and folly. And so, revelling and carousing the livelong night, and unwary of the future, they lived wedded to their pleasant vices.[9]

---

[7] For this thematic see app. 1.3.
[8] I find this, for example, in John of Dalyata, a Syrian author of the eigth century, Ep. 15,4 (PO 39, 348-49): "On account of pride we brought down the image of the Eternal King and we replaced it with an enormous idol of monstrous aspect so that the people come out of Egypt would worship it."
[9] De vita Mosis II 161 (OEuvres 22, p. 262; transl. F.H. Colson). Other passages in which Philo deals with Exod. 32 are: Spec. leg. 3, 215 (ibid. 25, p. 138); Ebr. 95 (ibid. 11-12, p. 62); Fug. 90 (ibid. 17, p. 166). See Pelletier (1966).

Jewish tradition had previously underlined the orgiastic aspects of the idolatrous cult,[10] but from the beginning of the second century, Christian commentators pursue this concern tenaciously. To them, instinctual pressure obstructed the correct knowledge and the correct cult. This line of reason had previously been taken up by Justin who, in meditating on God's accommodation to the needs and to the situation of the people, explains Jewish institutions thus:

> The very sabbath was therefore prescribed for you to remember God: this is what his Word means when he says: "so that you know that I am the God who has redeemed you." In fact, if he has forbidden you from eating certain foods it is so that even in eating and drinking you have God before your eyes, given your inclination and facility in giving up knowledge of him, as Moses also says: "The people ate and drank and rose to make revelry." And again: "Jacob ate, satisfied and fattened himself and resisted, the beloved; he stuffed himself, he became big and fat and abandoned the God who had made him."[11]

Nonetheless, as we can see, Justin's accent falls in quite a positive way on divine pedagogy, which in order to maintain Israel's attention directed to it, supplies concrete indications concerning food. There is also a similar insistence on pedagogy in Iraenaeus, who underlines, as Paul had done previously, the role of "lust."[12]

Analogous justifications of the Jewish prescriptions concerning worship are common among ancient Christian writers, but with significant differences and emphases according to area, and, above all, to time of writing and the worsening relationship with Judaism.[13] For this reason, there is increasing insistence, in ever stronger, more insulting terms, and with greater distance and inquisitorial coldness, on Jewish carnality as an insuperable obstacle to divine knowledge and as the fundamental element in the Jews' irreversible moral inferiority. While the tones of Clement of Alexandria are singularly moderate, Tertullian – in a different, Christian-latin, African environment – situates himself at the very origins of a moralistic tradition that finds in idolatry the consequence of carnal excesses: food, wine, sexual transgression. He writes:

> And if the law eliminated some food and declared unclean those animals which had previously been blessed, understand in that a plan to exercise continence and restraint on greed, because they, whilst

---

[10]For example ExR 32, 6 (478); see Smolar and Aberbach (1968) p. 104.
[11]Dial. 19, 6-20, 1 (Archambault, pp. 88-90).
[12]Adv. haer. IV 15, 1 (SC 100, 548-52) quoted later, note 77.
[13]See also Clement of Alexandria, Paed. II 1, 17 (GCS 12, 166); Novatianus, De cibis iud. 4 (CC 4, 96-97).

Jewish Carnality

eating the bread of the angels, desired the cucumbers and the melons of the Egyptians. Recognize in that a provision for the comrades of greed, that is to say, lust and lechery, which are usually calmed by punishing the belly: "the people had eaten," in fact, "they had drunk and had risen to make revelry" [Exod. 32:6]. In the same way, so that desire for money be suppressed by the motive that was adopted, that of the necessity of sustenance, luxury in exquisite foods was prohibited: finally, so that man might more easily be accustomed to fasting in honor of God, he was trained to eat few and not luxurious foods, under the order not to eat anything more refined.[14]

And African moralism fully exploits the link, frequent in the Bible, between idolatry and fornication.[15] It sees in *lusus* a sexual transgression to which the Bible only timidly alludes: "Scripture would not have spoken of 'game' if it had not been wanton," observes Tertullian (who also adds the quotation from Deut. 32:15, according to which Israel is the fatted calf, useless for work, useful only for the butcher).[16]

In the fourth century, the generalized advent of this type of moralism comes fully to bear on Judaism, the carrier par excellence of those base inclinations, of that dangerous instinctiveness that the Church, in the period of mass conversions had to face for the first time on a large scale. Voices multiply, but John Chrysostom's is heard above others. It says: "The Jews committed the worst sins, falling from drunkenness and excess of food into iniquity."[17] "Do you see the charges of excess in food that the prophet made to those insensible stubborn Jews

---

[14]Adv. Marc. II 18, 2 (CC 1, 495-96): "Et si lex aliquid cibis detraxit et inmunda pronuntiat animalia, quae aliquando benedicta sunt, consilium exercendae continentiae intellege et frenos impositos illi gulae agnosce, quae, cum panem ederet angelorum, cucumeres aegyptiorum desiderabat. Agnosce simul et comitibus gulae, libidini scilicet et luxuriae, prospectum, quae fere ventria castigatione frigescunt: manducaverat enim populus et biberat et surrexerat ludere; proinde, ut et pecuniae ardor restringeretur ex parte, qua de victus necessitate causatur, pretiosorum ciborum ambitio detracta est; postremo, ut facilius homo ad ieiunandum Deo formaretur, paucis et non gloriosis escis adsuefactus est, nihil de lautioribus esuriturus." See also Adv. iud. 3, 12-13 (CC 2, 1347) for the description of the traiterous people, in spite of its privileges: "Ad instar erat aeternitatis redactus, nec humanis passionibus contaminatus aut saeculi huius cibis pastus, sed angelorum manna bibatus satisque beneficiis Deo obligatus."

[15]See F. Hauk and S. Schultz, s.v. *porné*, in ThWzNT 6, 579 ff.

[16]Ieiun. 6, 2 (CC 2, 1262). Coherently, the text continues to stress the utility of fasting: "Ceterum cui (sc. Mose) cor erectum potius inveniebatur quam impinguatum."

[17]In Matt. hom. 13, 1 (PG 57, 210). On Chrysostom's anti-Jewish polemic, the most complete work is by Simon (1948) pp. 256 ff.

who every day stuffed themselves more."[18] The Jews concern themselves exclusively with the flesh, shorthand here for sexual activity, activity turned to procreation. Referring to a sapiential passage that reads "Do not desire a multitude of good-for-nothing children ... because it is better to die childless than to have impious children" (Sir. 16:1), and making a travesty of Mic. 2:15 (which is positive), Chrysostom observes: "But the insensible Jews, always chained to the flesh, and careless of virtue, said: 'What does God want, if not the seed.'"[19]

Cyril of Alexandria exemplifies a similar violence of abuse against the Jews when he states that their "lightness and paucity of spirit" depends on an innate tendency to passion which renders divine pedagogy useless.[20] Drawing his remarks from a prophetic text (Isa. 1:11-12), he underlines how the itinerary of ascent from creation to creator is impossible for a mind weighed down by the pleasures of the flesh – indeed, he claims the Jews gave themselves over to greed in order to avoid facing the future and the calamities that divine wrath was preparing. If they had given thought to the future, they would have given themselves over to works of penance.[21] John of Damuscus warns of the easy step which leads from excess in food to idolatry.[22] And Philoxenus of Mabbug, a monophysite Syrian writer of the fifth century, writes: "From love of the belly they have come to idolatry; from food to curses; from delights to all manner of evil."[23]

But it seems to me that the stereotypical contrast between Jewish carnality and Christian spirituality is formed mainly in Western and latin milieux, where it is elaborated principally in monastic terms. In addition to innumerable moral opinions, the African tradition also offered, by contrast, the motive of impatience. Indeed, it is impatience which marks the entire history of the people of Israel – their essential sin lies in their inability to respect God's time and his coming. This pattern, and its survival in later elaborations, can be traced from Tertullian[24] and Cyprian[25] to Ambrose[26] and Cassiodorus,[27] and on to

---

[18]In Gen. I hom. 1 (PG 53, 25).
[19]Exp. ps. 113,5 (PG 55, 312).
[20]De ador. Sp. et ver. I (PG 68, 143).
[21]In Isa. I or. 3 (PG 44, 149-51).
[22]In I Cor. 10, 6-7. (PG 95, 646; see 616). See also Oecumenius, Exp. I Cor. 10, 7 (PG 124, 682; see 712 and 777).
[23]Hom. IO, 403 (SC 44,359).
[24]Pat. 5, 22-25 (CC 1, 305-06): "An non ipsum quoque Israel per impatientiam semper in Deum deliquisse manifestum est? Exinde cum oblitus brachii caelestis quo aegyptiis adflictationibus fuerat extractus de Aaron deos sibi duces postulat, cum in idolum auri sui conlationes defundit: tam necessarias

Jewish Carnality 35

Peter Lombard.[28] Nonetheless, ancient Christian rhetoric (and here Ambrose is a prime example) aims rather at contrasting Moses, fasting "in superioribus montibus," to the people revelling at the banquet, participants in the orgy and the sacrilege "in inferioribus."[29] It contrasts the "ecclesia magna," the "populus gravis, non irriquietus et mobilis" to the Jewish "levitas";[30] the "mater fidei continentia" to the "perfidiae mater ebrietas"[31] ("those who begin to fall into lechery also stray from the faith");[32] the "synagoga meretrix procax" to the converted and faithful "ecclesia de prophanis."[33] With his usual self-congratulatory rigor, Jerome underscores the drunkenness-nudity-*libido-luxuria* process ("first the belly and then the rest")[34] and recalls the transgressions of Israel, combining the account in Exod. 32 with the powerful and realistic description of the prostitution of the virgin Israel in Ezek. 16.[35] In addressing the same issue, Augustine aims to edify the Christian community. Thus his reasoning tends to note not only the gravity, but also the exceptionality of the golden calf transgression and the excessive behaviour connected with it. In a

---

enim Moysi cum Domini congredientis impatienter exceperat moras. Post mannae escatilem pluviam, post petrae aquatilem sequellam desperant de Domino tridui sitim non sustinendo; nam haec quoque illis impatientia exprobatur. Ac ne singula pervagemur: numquam non per impatientiam delinquendo perierunt. Quomodo enim manus prophetis intulerunt nisi per impatientiam audiendi? Domino autem ipso per impatientiam etiam videndi. Quodsi patientiam inisset, liberarentur." See also Scorp. 3, 3 (CC 2, 1074).

[25]Bon. pat. 19 (CC 3A, 129): "Nonne quod a Deo primum recessit impatientiae crimen fuit? Dum Moysi cum Deo colloquentis moras non potest ferre, prophanos deos ausus est postulare, ut itineris sui duces nuncuparet caput bubulum et terrestre figmentum, nec umquam ab eadem impatientia destitit quominus semper docilitatis et divinae administrationis impatiens prophetas suos et iustos quosque ad crucem quoque et sanguinem Domini prosiliret. Impatientia etiam in ecclesia haereticos facit et ad iudaeorum similudinem contra Christi pacem et caritatem rebelles ad hostilia et furiosa bella compellit."

[26]De Helia et ieiun. 12, 41 (CSEL 32/2, 436).

[27]Exp. Ps. 105, 20 (CC 98, 965).

[28]Comm. Ps. 105, 19 (PL 191, 964).

[29]Ambrose, De Helia et ieiun. 6,16 (CSEL 32/2, 421): "Et in superioribus quidem montis lex dabatur Moysi ieiunanti, in inferioribus populo manducanti praevaricatio sacrilega luxu accendebatur epulantium."

[30]Exp. Ps. 39, 32 (CSEL 64, 228-29).

[31]De Helia ieiun. 12, 41 (CSEL 32/2, 436).

[32]Ep. 58, 16 (PL 16, 1232).

[33]Expl. Ps. 36, 6 (CSEL 64, 74).

[34]Ep. Ps.. 22, 8 (CSEL 54, 155).

[35]Ep. 79, 11 (CSEL 55, 100).

certain sense, I think he says, in their intoxication the Christian people are worse than this, the carnal people par excellence. With this admonition, Augustine aligns himself with the position expressed in Paul's speeches to the people at Corinth.[36]

The high medieval moralistic and spiritual reflection draws massively for its warnings on the idolatrous episode of Exod. 32. These warnings, however, have very little to do with Judaism. Rather, they bear directly on the various underlying vices of greed, drunkenness, *luxuria, voluptas.* "Voluptuousness is almost always a companion of the feasts," Gregory the Great comments at the end of the sixth century.[37] Clearly, for him *voluptas* is already a sin.

It is in this way, in an increasingly abstract and formal manner, that the elaboration of stereotypical Jewish carnality is continued. The logic is this: the Jews, who adored Priapus, have little reason to reprimand those who worship the crucifix.[38] The cultic worship which they rendered God was in fact impure, stained by *libido* and idolatrous leaning – their situation paralleled that of the man who knows his wife not through uxoral love but by *libido coeundi.*[39] That is, the prophetic criticism of official Judaism, including that from Jesus, consolidated gradually into a critique that fostered awareness of the signs and the times of God, removed nostalgia for the past and showed gratitude for the gifts of God. This led in turn to Christianity's definition of the Jew as a psychological type: carnal, a slave to instinct, unable to gain access to the elevated spiritual sphere on which the Christian experience (above all in its monastic mode) hinges.

We should note that the charge of avarice, although present, does not yet dominate in the portrait of the Jew. In the ecclesiastic literature on the subject, Jewish worship of the mammon gold is still a secondary concern.[40] However, the carnality that characterizes Christianity's

---

[36]Ep. 29.4 (CSEL 34/1,115-16); see also Ep. 36, 15 (CSEL 34/2, 43-44).

[37]Mor. Iob. I 8, 10 (CC 143, 29).

[38]See Gilbert of Nogent, De incarn. adv. iud. III 9 (PL 156, 525).

[39]See William of Melitona, Quaest. sacram. I 5, 28,4c (ed. Piana, Quaracchi 1961, vol. 1, p. 119): "Unde non offerebant principaliter ut oboedirent Deo et ob devotionem divini cultus, sed ex quadam libidine et pronitate superstitionis cultus idolorum; sic quando quis conoscit suam non affectu uxorio, sed libidine coeundi."

[40]Some traces, but which are not as significant as might be expected, of this direction are hinted at. For Origen, the Egyptian gold is still false wisdom (see above, note 2); Cyprian of Carthage (Ad. Nov. 1, 6; CC 4, 138) speaks of the gold "in quo prima delicta populi denotata sunt." I find little evidence of the golden calf-Mammon link: see, however, Martyrius (Sahdona), Libr. perf. I 4, 3, 34 (CSCO 201, 117). From the making of the calf it emerges that "auri cupiditas materiam esse perfidiae, et avaritiae studio sacrilegia solere generari," but

definition of the Jew is tied tightly to lust, to *epithymia*, to the instinctual sphere. But this is a biblical cliché prior to Christianity. It appears in the tradition of the murmuring in the desert (Num. 11, Ps. 105), the New Testament elaboration of certain aspects contained in Stephen's speech (Acts 7), and Paul's warning (1 Cor. 10). The Bible suggests forgetfulness of divine benefits and nostalgia for Egypt as motives for the idolaters. Indeed, the charges of Israel's forgetfulness and ingratitude recur in Jewish Scripture from Deuteronomy to the prophets to Nehemiah. And it is from here that they pass to the New Testament literature, to post-biblical authors and the Koran.[41]

Ambrose (Apol. proph. David I 4 and 17; CSEL 32/2, 310) is worried above all by the warning given to the Christian people. So is Peter Chrysologus, Serm. 29 (PL 52, 282). On the other hand, the link between avarice and idolatry, idolorum servitus, previously put forward by the New Testament (Col. 3:5; Ef 5:5), is not often associated with the Jewish people: this does not happen, for example, in Aimone of Halberstadt, In Gal. 5 (PL 117, 692) and In. Ep. 5 (PL 117, 725); in Atto of Vercelli, In. Col. *ad. loc.* (PL 134, 632); in Rudolph Ardens, Hom. 39 (PL 155,1804); in Bruno the Carthusian, In Ep. ad. loc. (PL 153, 343) = In Col., *ad. loc.* (ibid., 391). There are some polemical remarks: Aaron yields "partim coactus, partim cupiditate pecuniae" (Haimo of Halberstadt, Expl. Ps. 105, 20; PL 116, 559); "cupidi et avari (Bruno of Segni, Exp. Exod. 32; PL 164, 368). There is nothing to compare with what was to happen later, nothing comparable to the violence against the Jews and their avidity of wealth found in the Lutheran pamphlet *Against the Jews and their Lies* (1543): these are stereotypes that are carried forward upto Marx's *On the Jewish Question* (1843), where the violent critique of Judaism seems to have a basis in the discovery and the Marxian denunciation of the role of the bourgeoisie: see the conclusions to the present work.

[41]Justin lists among the benefits: the division of the Red Sea, the column of fire, Mara's waters, quayles, prophetic signs like the bronze serpent and Moses' open arms, Meriba's waters, cloud, clothes that do not wear out: "and instead of all this you made the calf and you fornicated with the daughters of the foreigners and you tried to engage in idolatry" (Dial. 131-32; Archambault, pp. 270-74). This is a complicated list, which also unites, among the benefits and transgressions, elements which come historically after the account given in Exod. 32. Simpler listings are found in other apologists and theologians. Tertullian: crossing of the Red Sea, crossing of the desert, manna: "satisque beneficiis Deo obligatus, Domini et Dei sui oblitus est" (Adv. iud. 3, 12-13; CC 2, 1347). The pseudoclementine *Recognitiones*: ten plagues, the Red sea, manna, water from the rocks, cloud and column of fire, apostasy (Recogn. I 35, 1-5; GCS 51, 29). Origen: signs and portents in Egypt, Red Sea, column of fire and cloud, gift of the law, *apistia* (C. Cels. II 74; SC 132, 460). *Didascalia apostolorum*: Moses' prodigious acts, ten plagues, Red Sea, Mara's waters, water from the rock, fire and cloud, quayles, gift of the law: "hunc [God] denegaverunt dicentes: 'Non hebemus deum qui praecedat nos'" (Did. ap. 26; Connolly, p. 221; CSCO 408, 226; see also Did. ap. 23). There are similar listings in 4 Esdra, whose invective begins with "obliti enim sacrificaverunt diis alienis" and continues with the contraposition of benefits and betrayals in a form that

Nevertheless, in the post-biblical Christian polemic Jewish carnality becomes an attribute characterizing Jewish stock, making it irreducibly different from its Christian counterpart. The Jews suffer under a hereditary trait and deficiency incompatible with Christian spirituality.

In the same way, the evocation of the regressive drive back to Egypt, an Old and New Testament theme (Stephen's discourse), is transformed into a heavy indictment of the Egyptian origins of Jewish idolatry. Not only do Christian writers once again take up Egypt's desire for material goods from the Old Testament,[42] they also soon assert that the idol itself is Egyptian.[43] Indeed, the Egyptian god Apis is often depicted as the divinity worshipped at the foot of Mt. Sinai.[44]

---

influenced the impropreria of Roman liturgy. See Schmidt (1957) pp. 794 ff. Similar listings are in Eusebius of Emesa, Opusc. 10, 6-7 (Buytaert, vol. 1, pp. 242 ff); Asterius of Amaseia, with invectives directed against the Jews of his time, "incredulous children of incredulous fathers" (Or. 7; PG 40, 260-62). Jewish forgetfullness and ingratitude are insistent themes in John Chrysostom: Adv. iud. 5, 4 (PG 48, 889); frequent forgetfullness by the Jews: De poenit. hom. 6, 2 (PG 49, 301); Jews who are "insensitive and ungrateful"; De prod. Iudae 1, 4 (PG 49, 379); Quod nemo laeditur nisi a seipso 13 (PG 52, 475); In Gen. I hom. 1, 4 (PG 53, 25); Cat. 5, 16-18 (SC 50, 208-10). See also Theodore of Mopsuestia, In. Os. 7, 13-16 (PG 66, 169) where God speaks in the first person. There is a long list of benefits, to which is opposed the ingratitude of the "stock hostile to God and resistent to the divine benefits" in Basil of Seleucia, Or. 31, 1 (PG 85, 340-41). See also in Anastasius Sinaita the invectives against blindness, stubbornness, ingratitude etc. (Disp. adv. iud. II; PG 89, 1235). Also in Ephraem, see Serm. 2, 553-57 (CSCO 312, 68). In the West, see Ambrose, Expl. Ps. 38, 3 (CSEL 64, 186); Augustine, In. Io. III 19 (CC 36, 29); Cromatius, Serm. 9, 2 (SC 154, 198); later, Rupert of Deutz, In Mich. 3 (PL 168, 503-05) there is a long development of the "popule meus, quid feci tibi" (Mic 6, 3-5) with the invitation "non sit in nobis cor durum et indomabile et ferrea cervix."

[42]As, for example, in Jerome, In Am. II 5, 25-27 (CC 76, 297): "Semper corde reversi sunt in Aegyptum, desiderantes allia et cepe et cucumeres et carnes aegyptias et manna, quae de caelo est, contemnentes" (see Num. 11).

[43]Ancient Rabbinic sources are ignorant of this location: see Ginzburg, *Legends*, vol. 6, note 271; it is found in Rashi, recalled by Nicholas of Lyra, *ad loc*.

[44]In Philo, however, something similar is found: the Jews make an "imitation of the animal that passes as the most sacred in the country" (De vita Mosis II 162; Oeuvres 22, p. 262). Such identification is very common in Christian milieux. Recogn. I 34, 5 (GCS 51, 28): "secundum speciem Apidis, quem coli in Aegypto viderant"; Lactantius, Div. inst. IV 10, 12 (CSEL 19, 303): "aureum caput bovis, quem vocant Apim"; Const. ap. V 12, 2 (Funk, p. 267); Cyril of Alexandria, Glaph. Exod. III (PG 69, 528); pseudo-Chrysostom, In Ps. 105, 3 (PG 55, 662); Procopius of Gaza, Comm. Exod. 20, 9 and 32, 1 (PG 87/1, 607 and 663), without specifying Apis; Anastasius Sinaita, Dial. parv. ad iud. (PG 89, 1273): in Egypt the Jews worshipped various animals; Ephraem, Hymn. 87, 4 (CSCO 155, 228): Egyptian

And from the beginning of the second century, Christian writers talk of a calf's head as a more accurate object of idolatrous worship.[45] Could this accusation not be a reprisal, perhaps, for the charge of zoolatry

---

origin of the cult of the calf; Iso'dad of Merv, Comm. Exod. 32, 1-4 (CSCO 179, 73). In the West, the Glossa ordinaria spreads this belief which was previously present in Jerome, In Os. II 7, 15-16 (CC 76, 81): "ad similitudinem vituli, scil. bovis Apis, quem in Aegypto coluerunt" (PL 113, 286); Nicholas of Lyra, ad. loc., reports, without comment, Rashi's opinion on the presence of Egyptians among the Jews; but a later Additio confutes Rashi's opinion. William of Auvergne puts forward the Egyptian cult of Serapide or the astrological sign of the bull as models (De leg. 26; Opera omnia, Paris 1674, vol. 1, pp. 82 ff.). Luther shared this conviction, but traced Egyptian idolatry back to a perversion of the true cult learned by Joseph: "Aegypti cultum vitulorum e Ioseph patriarcha habent, quem videntes immolare Deo boves et vitulos, imitati sunt illum. Omnis idolatria ex fide et religione vera fluit" (Tischr. 767; WA 1, 367). They still thought that the golden calf was the Egyptian Apis, In I Cor. 10 (Opera 15, 1099); Calvin (Opera 25, Corp. ref. 55, 83); Cornelius a Lapide, In Exod., *ad loc.* (Comm. Pent., Antwerp 1648, p. 577); Estius, Annotationes, *ad loc.* (Antwerp 1699, p. 51); Grotius, Ad Exod., *ad loc.* (*Opera omnia theologica*, Amsterdam 1679, p. 57); Reimarus, Apol. I 3 ,5 (ed. G. Alexander, Frankfurt 1972, p. 374); and the polyglot Bible of the Vigouroux (1900) ad loc. But present day exegesis does not hold this position, and the most correct thesis on the symbolic meaning of the bull is still that previously found in Monceius, *Aaron expurgatus* (Atrebati 1606) [see Childs (1974) pp. 574 ff.] and in H. More, *Modesta inquisitio* V I (Opera omnia, London 1675, pp. 457 ff.).

[45]*Caput vituli*: Recogn. I 34,5 (GCS 51, 28); *bubulum caput*: Tertullian, Adv. iud. 1, 5 (CC 2, 1340); Cyprian, Bon. pat. 19 (CC 3A, 129); *pecudis caput*: Origen, In Num. hom. 3, 2 (GCS 30, 16); again Origen, *caput vituli* (In Exod. hom. 13, 5; GCS 29, 277); Gregory of Nazianzus, *kephale tou moschou* (Or. 45, 16; PG 36, 645); Eusebius of Emesa, *caput vituli* (Opusc. 10, 7; Buytaert, vol. 1, p. 242); John Chrysostom, Quod nemo laeditur 13 (PG 52, 476); pseudo-Chrysostom, C. iud. (PG 48, 1079): *boukefalon*; similarly, Leontius of Byzantium, Hom. 1, 8 (SC 187, 380; see M. Aubineau's note, ibid., p. 403 with other texts pertinent to the previously cited note); John of Damascus, Imag. 2, 8; 3, 5 (Kotter, p. 75) and Theodore Prodromus, Tetrast. V.T. (PG 133, 1125): *boukranon*. Nicetas Choniates, Disc. 1 and 16 (ed. van Dieten, Berlin and New York 1972, pp. 104 and 182): *taurokranon*. See also Nicephorus Callistus, Syn. s. Script., *ad loc.* (PG 147, 509). Turning back to Western milieux, the formula caput vituli is the most constant: see Ambrose, Apol. David I 4,17 (CSEL 32/2, 310); Ep. 66,2 (PL 16, 1278); Expl. Ps. 36, 6 (CSEL 64, 74); Jerome, Ep. 77, 4 (CSEL 55, 40); Sulpicius Severus, Chron. I 19 (CSEL 1, 21); Peter Chrysologus, Serm. 29 (PL 52, 282, with editor's note); Rupert of Deutz, *caput vituli—capita draconis* from Ps. 73, 14: De s. Trin. 13, In Exod. IV 26 (CC cont. med. 22, 783), and various other texts. Finally, Peter Comestor is more prudent: "Tradunt quidam Aaron proiecisse in ignem inaures, et inde opere daemonis conflatum caput vituli tantum, quod tamen quandoque vitulus, quandoque caput vituli vocatur, quia in excusationem sui inferius legitur Aaron dixisse Moysi: 'Proieci illud in ignem et egressus est hic vitulus'" (Hist. schol.: Lib. Exod. 73; PL 198, 1189-90).

previously levelled at the Jews by the pagans and which was also directed at Christians?

In the patristic indictment, the image which best sums up the carnal nature of Israel is that of the calf, for the calf stands not only as an object of veneration but as a symbol of Israel itself – an Israel that has become that which it elected as its insignia and idol. In Deuteronomy we read: "Jacob ate and satiated himself – you fattened yourself, stuffed yourself – and rejected God who made him, scorned the rock of his salvation" (32:15).[46] This is often likened to the evocation of the charge of idolatry leveled at the foot of Mt. Sinai that is already present in Justin and Tertullian,[47] but is found above all in Chrysostom. Chrysostom recuperates it in order to suggest the bestial condition to which Israel has been reduced in its disobedience, and the tragic consequences that follow:

> "You have broken, he says [Jer. 2; 20], the yoke," you did not only reject it: this is the vice of animals without reason who kick back, who reject restraint and refuse authority. But where does this stubbornness come from? From too much food and intoxication. Who says this? Moses himself: "Israel ate, filled and fattened itself and the beloved turned back." Like animals without reason, who have received food in plenty, having stuffed themselves, they become evasive and untamable and no longer tolerate the yoke nor the brake, nor the hand of the charioteer. So, the Jewish people out of intoxication and obesity fell into the worst of sins, rebelled, did not want to receive the yoke of Christ, nor draw the plough of discipline [and he quotes Hos. 4:16; Jer. 31:18]. But these brute animals unsuitable for work, become suitable for the slaughterhouse. Christ said: "My enemies, who did not want me to reign over them, bring them here and kill them."[48]

So an analysis of the idolatrous attitude ultimately reveals the stereotype of Israel's bestiality. The Jews become "people of slow minds and of a truly bestial obstinacy."[49] And analogous hostile formulas, full of threats and destructiveness, arise. Evidently, wherever the prophetic invective (including that of the New Testament) found in the

---

[46] According to the Septuagint. The Masoretic text omits "Jacob....satiated" and adds "Iesurum fattened himself and kicked back," a term which alludes to the bull.

[47] Justin, Dial. 20, 1 (Archambault, p. 92); Tertullian, Ieiun. 6, 2-5 (CC 2, 1262).

[48] Adv. iud. 1,2 (PG 48, 846). See also John Chrysostom, Catech. 5, 16-17 (SC 50, 208): Exod. 32 plus Deut. 32,15; the same coupling In Gen. hom. 1, 2 (PG 47, 23). Similarly, Ambrose, Expl. ps. 38, 34 (CSEL 64, 209); Jerome, Adv. Iov. II 15 (PL 23, 320); Augustine, Ep. 36, 7.15 (CSEL 34/2, 43); Philossenus of Mabbug, Hom. 10, 403-05 (SC 44, 359-61).

[49] Peter of Blois, C. perf. iud. I (PL 207, 827): "...populo durae cervicis atque pertinaciae vere bestialis"; Peter the Venerable, Tract. c. iud. III (PL 189, 539): "Quamdiu, o iudaei, hic bovinus intellectus cordibus vestris insederit?"

Jews a form of self-sufficiency, of confidence in themselves, of "boastfulness" which might prevent the reception of the innovatory elements introduced by the prophets,[50] it levels the charge of carnality, attributing to the Jew inhuman and bestial characteristics in order to degrade him as an adversary.

Only the Lutheran critique of these works brings a vigorous correction to this perspective, recovering a biblically correct idea of carnality. Here we read: "The term 'flesh' is thus obscured by Papists, for whom flesh means laying together and the satisfaction of desire: but here the work of the flesh is idolatry, the highest and greatest point of human wisdom."[51] In other words, the greatest point of religiosity and spirituality is the work of the flesh, and not simple sexual practice (here Luther refers to Gal. 5:20). But the full application of such reasoning to Judaism, the correction of the stereotype of carnality, the understanding, that is, of Judaism as a dimension immanent in Christianity itself, are, it would seem, only recent achievements and certainly are not widely shared.[52]

The idea of Jewish carnality survives in Feuerbach's critique in *Das Wesen des Christentums* (1841). For Feuerbach, the essence of Judaism is egotism, utilitarianism, sensuality, visceralness:

> The Greeks looked on nature in a theoretical sense: they perceived celestial music in the harmonious progress of the stars; they saw nature rise from the spray of the ocean which generates all, in the likeness of Venus Anadiomene. The Jews opened only their gastric senses to nature: only in the palate did they find the taste of nature, only eating the manna did they become aware of their God: "*At sunset you will eat* meat and in the morning *you will satisfy yourselves with bread and you will know* that *I am the Lord* your God [Exod. 16:12: original italics]. Eating is the most solemn act or even the initiation of the Jewish religion. In eating the Israelite celebrates and renews the act of creation; in eating man understands nature as an *object which itself is nothing*. When the seventy elders climbed the mountain with Moses, "*they saw God and although they saw God they drank and ate.*" The sight of the supreme being caused only appetite in them.[53]

And Hegel had previously remarked on these same sensual aspects: "The three great annual feasts that were celebrated with banquets and dances are the most human element of Moses' legislation." However an even clearer clue to the low, passive, almost purely vegetative level of

---

[50]In Gal. comm. 5, 20 (WA 40/2, 211-12).
[51]In Gal. comm. 5, 20 (WA 40/2, 211-12).
[52]I am thinking of the pages which Karl Barth dedicates to the theme in *Kirchliche Dogmatik* (1953) pp. 470 ff.
[53]Feuerbach (1841) pp. 205 ff. One of Feuerbach's sources is the anti-Jewish tract by J.E. Eisenmenger, *Entdecktes Judentum* (Frankfurt 1700).

the Jewish condition, says Hegel, is the feast of the sabbath, with the sloth that it brings: "In this complete passivity, beyond the testimony of their slavery, there remains for them nothing but the mere and empty need to maintain their physical existence and to make it safe. Therefore, when they had achieved their physical existence with their lives, they wanted nothing more."[54]

3. A Servile People

The young Hegel underlines the servile character of this people. They are "without a soul and without any need for freedom." He writes: "The liberator of the people was also its legislator. This could only mean that he had freed them from one yoke and had forced another on them."[55] Another stereotype, the "servile" people, now accompanies the carnal stereotype. And underlying both is the idea of an inferior, almost animal existence which can be controlled and harnessed only by the severity of a law, and from which only Christianity can guarantee respite.

The idea of a necessary servile condition for the Jews, against which is posited Christian liberty, has a long history in the Pauline debate. It appears most prominently in the Letters to the Romans and Galatians. The Christians, says Paul, are children of Abraham and of Sarah, the free woman; they are, that is, the progeny of Isaac. By contrast, the Jews are the children of Abraham and of Hagar, the slave woman, the progeny of Ishmael. He writes:

> It is written that Abraham had two sons, one of the slave woman, and one of the free woman. But the son born of the slave woman was born according to the flesh; the son born of the free woman, in virtue of the promise. Now, such things are spoken in allegory: the two women represent the two covenants. The one on Mt. Sinai which generates slavery, represented by Agar (Sinai is a mountain in Arabia); it corresponds to the present Jerusalem, which is a slave

---

[54]Hegel (1907) pp. 176.

[55]Ibid., p. 174. Spinoza expresses a similar position, Tract. theol.-polit. II: "Israelitae de Deo nihil fece norunt, tametsi ipsis revelatus est, quod quidem plusquam satis ostenderunt, cum ejus honorem, et cultum paucis post diebus vitulo tradiderunt, credideruntque illum esse eos deos, qui eos ex Aegypto eduxerant. Nec sane credendum est, quod homines superstitionibus aegyptiorum assueti, rudes, et miserrima servitute confecti, aliquid sani de Deo intellexerint, aut quod Moses eos aliquid docuerit, quam modum vivendi, non quidem tanquam philosophus, ut tandem ex animi libertate, sed tanquam Legis lator, ut ex imperio Legis coacti essent bene vivere. Quare ratio bene vivendi, sive vera vita, Deique cultus, et amor iis magis servitus, quam vera libertas, Deique gratia, et donum fuit" (Opera, Heidelberg 1924, vol. 3, pp. 40 ff).

together with its sons. The Jerusalem above is free and is our mother (Gal. 4:22-26).

The Christian tradition fully exploits this suggestion (which needs to be broadened to take account of the context of the Pauline debate on the law). It fixes its attention on the events of Sinai and on the two successive covenants separated by the idolatry of the people and the breaking of the first tablets. Among the many consequences of the worship of the golden calf are the immediate punishment of the guilty (on which I shall presently elaborate) and, after the pardon, the consequence of the gift of the new tablets. Christian tradition focuses on the problem of the nature of the second tablets or "second law," the law which God gives to the people (*deuterosis*)[56] for the second time. Christian considerations of the problem produce different positions in which are reflected the many attitudes and perplexities of the ancient church when faced with the ethical/moral aspect of Jewish Scriptures that the Church had always accepted and venerated.

One early point of view ignores the second tablets on principle. This position is expressed in the Epistle of Barnabas. As we have seen, according to Barnabas' Epistle, by turning to the idol, the Israelites lost the pact "when Moses received it": "Moses understood and threw the two tablets away from his hands and their covenant was broken, in order that the covenant of Jesus, the beloved, could be sealed in our hearts, in the hope of faith in him." "He gave it, but they were not worthy of receiving it ... Moses then received it, but they were not worthy of it."[57] No mention here of the renewal of the covenant (which Exod. 34 establishes).

From this perspective, all the ethical/ritual dispositions have a purely spiritual sense; they stand for the church as prefigurations of eschatological realities, while the actual practice of the dispositions on the part of the Jewish people is to be and was condemned from the outset as the work of the devil:

> The circumcision in which they held faith was refused. In fact, he did not speak of a circumcision of the flesh: but they transgressed, deceived by a fallen angel. To them he says: "Your Lord God says these things (here I find the commandment): 'Do not sow seeds among the thorns, circumcise yourselves for your Lord.' And what does he say? "Circumcise the hardness of your hearts and do not thicken your heads" [Deut. 10, 16]. Furthermore: "Here, says the Lord, all people are uncircumcised in the flesh, but this people remained uncircumcised in the heart" [Jer. 9, 24-25]. You may say: but that people was circumcised as a sign. But even every Arab and Syrian and

---

[56]Simon (1948) pp. 114-17; Bietenhard (1957).
[57]Ep. Barn. 4, 8 and 14, 1.4.

all the priests of the idols are circumcised. Even they are part of their covenant. Even the Egyptians are circumcised.[58]

Here, the norms of the ancient covenant are deprived of any function other than that of leading back to the realities of Christ and the church. Indeed, they paradoxically serve to condemn those who want to put them into practice by placing them at the same level as the Gentiles (this is a travesty of Paul's thought, of the dialectic that he elaborates between holiness and necessity of the law, on the one hand, and its ineffectiveness for salvation on the other).

A less radical and more historicized position admits the second law, but underlines its repressive function after the people's transgression. This position is represented in its clearest form in *Didascalia Apostolorum*. It gains weight and influence when passed on to the *Constitutiones Apostolorum*. Not surprisingly, its major point is the distinction between law and reiteration of the law (*secundatio legis, deuterosis*). The former is the decalogue, the "simple, salubrious, healthy" law which Jesus himself confirms and which is *indestructibilis*, indissoluble. This law precedes the apostasy of the golden calf. It comprises "The law and the decalogue and the judgments [Exod. 20-21] that the Lord communicated before the people made the calf and fell into idolatry.... The law ... is simple and straightforward, it does not contain onerous preparations of food, nor sacrifices, nor the burning of offerings." (At the most, this law allows those who so wish freely to make sacrifices, as is the case for Cain, Abel and Noah.)[59] This law is the natural law, according to the rereading of *Constitutiones Apostolorum*.[60] By contrast, the second law is born of anger. Despite all the divine gifts the Jews had received, "they made sacrifices to a statue, and so the Lord was enraged and in the tumult of his anger, together with his great mercy, disciplined them with the repetition of the law and with the imposition of the weight and the gravity of the chain."[61] These burdens comprise the restrictions on food and worship that the prophets criticized strongly and which the Saviour will come to take away. Here, clarifies the *Constitutiones*

---

[58]Ibid. 9, 4.

[59]Did. ap. 26 (Connolly, pp. 217-21; CSCO 408, 223-26): "Lex ergo et decalogus et iudicia [Exod. 20-21], quae antequam vitulum faceret populus et idolatraret locutus est dominus ... Lex autem simplex est et levis, non habens onerantes parationes escarum neque sacrificia neque combustionum oblationes."

[60]Const. ap. VI 20, 1 (Funk, p. 349); see VI 20, 4 (p. 351): *physikos nomos*.

[61]Did. ap. 26 (Connolly, p. 230; CSCO 408, 226): "Sacrificaverunt sculptili. Propterea iratus est dominus et in furore irae suae, cum misericordia bonitatis suae, alligavit illos in secundatione legis et adstrictione oneris et duritia catanae."

Jewish Carnality

Apostolorum, the restrictions, not the natural law, are concerned.[62] To underline the repressive function of the second law, a passage from Ezekiel is quoted: after the many transgressions, God says: "then I gave them bad statutes and laws according to which they could not live" (20:25).[63]

The same quotation, with the same function, appears in Iraenaeus and in Aphraates, a Syrian theologian of the fourth century.[64] And a similar point of view appears in a text which also comes from Jewish/Christian milieux, the pseudoclementine *Recognitiones*. It speaks of a compromise with a *novella institutio* following the betrayal that aimed at fighting the *mala vetustae consuetudinis* (the habit, brought from Egypt, of sacrificing idols). The compromise allows the immolation of victims but only when dedicated to the true God. This allows evil, the "ancient vice," to be immediately cast out yet in part conserves it so that it may be completely expelled by the Prophet whose coming Moses himself announces.[65]

Tertullian is very harsh in his treatment of the Jews. We have already seen in his *Adversus iudaeos* how the apostasy of the golden calf – as such, or as it is repeated through time – becomes, without any other more complete historical mediation, the cause of Israel's and the people's rejection of the calling: "Make us gods ... and *therefore* we became his people."[66] We have seen how, for Tertullian, "it is proven that they are *always* considered guilty of the crime of idolatry as is documented by the divine Scriptures."[67] Yet, in the polemic against Marcion (an enemy of the Old Testament), and in the moralistic transposition of Jewish notions and precepts, Tertullian was ready to recognize the still relevant historical and pedagogical meaning of the harsh discipline imposed by the law which followed the idolatry.[68]

---

[62]Const. ap. VI 22, 5 (Funk, p. 357): *epeisakta*.
[63]Did. ap. 26 (Connollly, p. 230; CSCO 408, 2 31-32).
[64]Respectively Adv. haer. IV 15,1 (SC 100, 550), of which more later, and Dem. 15, 7 (PS 1/1, 753-56). Aphraates states: "At praecepta et iudicia vivifica ea sunt superius sunt conscripta; iudicia iusta et recta quae coram eis posuit, sunt decem mandata sancta, quae manu sua exaravit, Moysique tradidit ut doceret illos. Cum autem sibi finxissent vitulum, et a Deo recessissent, tunc illis dedit praecepta et iudicia non bona, sacrificium ac purgationem leprae, et profluvii, et menstruae, et partus" (trans. R. Graffin).
[65]Recogn. I 35, 6 (GCS 51, 29). For a similar point of view in Origen, Lev. cat. 1,2 (PG 12, 397).
[66]Adv. iud. 3, 13 (CC 2,1 347) cited above.
[67]Ibid. 1, 7 (1340).
[68]The law restrains greed, lust, luxury and avarice, according to the previously cited text Adv. Marc. II 18,2 (CC 1, 495). For the urgency of a discipline to restrain greed see: Ieiun. 6, 2-5 (CC 2, 1262).

We are faced, then, in the texts to which I have referred, with an oscillation between an invitation to repression and the recognition of the pedagogical utility of the repressive norms – from slavery to liberty is the underlying itinerary. It seems, however, that from the beginning of the fourth century, the further sedimentation of the two major actors' positions (caused by the irresistible advance of Christianity) means, among other things, that a blind eye is turned to the providential and pedagogical dimensions of the law, to which I shall return shortly. In this way, the motive of "Jewish servitude" takes center stage. Gradually, it becomes a justification for the Jews' oppression under judicial and social statutes. It blends with the pagan common-place of the "nation made for slavery."[69] Indeed, the two themes of servitude to the law and to politics intertwine so that it is difficult at a certain historical moment to distinguish the one from the other.[70]

Even where the theme of a necessary calling to political servitude does not emerge forcefully, Christian tradition nonetheless seems to insist on the repressive rather than the educative aspects of the Torah. It argues that the servile nature of the Jewish people "prefers the slavery of Egypt to the freedom of the faith,"[71] and on these grounds justifies treating the Jewish people with the "iron fist of the king."[72] Thus the pseudo-Augustine speaks of *gravia praecepta* given after the breaking of the tablets without referring to the positive aspects (except, of course, the figural value of the norms concerning the sabbath and circumcision).[73] Similarly, in dealing with the problem of the concession to offer sacrifices which is made to the people, Anastasius Sinaita brings up texts already mentioned in the *Constitutiones Apostolorum* (VI 20) and refers, above all, to the passage from Ezekiel concerning the "not good precepts." He comments: "They are not precepts worthy of my mercy nor of the good yoke that I wanted to impose on

---

[69] See Juster (1914) vol. 1, pp. 46 ff. To be sure, according to the Christian tradition, slavery is not only an effect of idolatrous sin, but also and above all of the crucifixion of the Son of God. The Jewish tradition attributes the loss of political freedom to the sin of Israel (above all the idolatrous sin), but obviously does not make any link with the repressive and punitive aspects of the Biblical law.

[70] See the treatment of the three slaveries of Israel in John Chrysostom, Adv. iud. 5, 5 (PG 48, 890-92).

[71] Chromatius, Serm.9, 2(SC 154,1 98).

[72] Asterius of Amaseia, Or. 7 (PG 40, 261).

[73] Lib. quaest. 44, 3 (CSEL 50, 73): "Quando simulacrum vituli fecerunt, tunc testamentum corruperunt. Unde et tabulae in quibus data lex fuerat, sub monte confractae sunt ex eo quod gravis praecepta meruerunt accipere."

Jewish Carnality 47

them and make them take up; they are harsh and necessary and adequate not to the mildness of the legislator, but to the insolence of the subjects."[74] Here it is interesting to observe how Anastasius denies the accommodation that had appeared essential to the first theologians in order to understand the nature of the second law.[75]

We have seen, now, how the stereotype of the Jewish law gradually grows and rigidifies into pure repression of the people, who deserve nothing less than moral and political servitude. The same process occurs over a much shorter span of time in the Koran. Here, one passes from a positive consideration of the people as holder of the Book to a more analytic and inquisitorial evaluation of Jewish restrictions as punishment. We read: "this we did as punishment for their prevarication" (sura 6:146), and "finally, for the impiety of these Jews we have prohibited them the good things that they were once allowed and because they have strayed from God's path" (sura 4:160: the issue of usury is here at stake).

But let us return to Christianity. Although more and more common, the thread that interprets the precepts *post reatum vituli* in a repressive key is by no means unique. Another thread, which has equally ancient antecedents, if less historical persistence, also deserves mention. This is the point of view elaborated in the course of the 2nd century during a more direct and sharper debate with, on the one hand, Judaism and, on the other, gnosis and its negation of Jewish Scriptures (Iraenaeus, Clement). Here the repressive element, in the judgment of the *deuterosis*, is also present, but the historical consideration of the

---

[74]Quaest. 46 (PG 89, 600).
[75]We find the same recourse to this text in Rupert of Deutz, a medieval witness of the most ancient tradition. "Si rite consideres legis ordinem, postquam praecepta bona data sunt, quae faciens homo viveret in eis, istae caerimoniae praeceptaque non bona, in quibus non viverent, a reatu vituli sumpserunt initium, et hoc erat iugum gravissimum"(In Cant. I 1,6; CC cont. med. 26, 23). "Hoc fuit pactum vitae et pacis. Quae autem post vituli reatum mandavit non pertinent ad pactum vitae et pacis" (In Mal. 2; PL 168, 824). "Eatenus Moyses populo non velata facie bona et vitalia Dei praecepta dederat. Deinde subintroeunte reatu vituli, faciem eius velari oportuit, quando loquebatur ad populum"(De vict. verbi Dei IX 31; PL 169, 1422). That the repressive *deuterosis* is later contained in the canonic Book of Deuteronomy was an untenable position and in fact was not held, except for the Dialogus Timothei et Aquilae (77r; Conybeare, p. 66). It is, on the other hand, correctly held that "deuteronomy" is a title that depends on the reiteration of the law, but is not tied in any strict sense to the deuterosis (Exod. 34): see Origen, for example, In Gen. hom. 9.1 (GCS 29, 88); Hippolytus, fragment in GCS 1/2, 108; Augustine, Quaest. Deut. 48 (CC 33, 304): "Magis illius repetitio quam aliquid aliud; pauca enim sunt, quae ibi non sint, quod primum datum est."

situation of the people prevails over the moralistic and punitive elements.

For example, Justin sees in the dispositions which followed the breaking of the tablets an accommodation (*harmosamenos*) by God to the conditions of the people. It is in this sense that he interprets the concession to allow sacrifices in honor of God, the obligation to observe the sabbath and the equally directive food restrictions (given to the people so that they do not fall once again into idolatry and remember him even while eating and drinking).[76] The same idea of accommodation also appears in Iraenaeus. At first, the people are asked to observe natural precepts, the decalogue and nothing more: "God initially limited himself to recalling the natural precepts he had inscribed in the men when he made them gifts: the decalogue, without which no-one can be saved." But when the sin of idolatry is broached, God imposes on them for their *concupiscentia* an extra law, one that makes them for the moment more suitable for slavery than for liberty and which, although it does not separate them from him, ties them to the yoke of obedience. Iraenaeus writes, as we know:

> But when they turned to making the idol and returned in their souls to Egypt, desiring to be slaves rather than free people, consonant to their avidity, they received all the remaining slavery, which, while not sepating them from God, tamed them with a yoke of servitude. Ezekiel the prophet thus explains the cause of the legislation: "Their eyes followed the desire of their hearts and I gave them precepts which were not good and prescriptions according to which they could not live"(Ezek. 20:24-25).[77]

Here, the harsh judgment on idolatry and lust is by no means absent, nor is the conviction that slavery suited the Jewish people. Yet the general sense of the reasoning is more historicized. This is not an alien people, radically inferior, destined for slavery because they have been irresistibly drawn to idolatry. Rather, this people is part of the very same human reality to which the Church, the work of God, belongs. A

---

[76]Dial. 19, 6-20, 1 (Archambault, pp. 88-93).
[77]Adv. haer. IV 15, 1 (SC 100, 548-52): "Nam Deus primo quidem per naturalia praecepta quae ab initio infixa dedit hominibus admonens eos, hoc est per decalogum – quae si quis non fecerit, non habet salutem – et nihil plus ab eis exquisivit ... At ubi conversi sunt in vituli factionem et reversi sunt animis suis in Aegyptum, servi pro liberis concupiscentes esse, aptam concupiscentiae suae acceperunt reliquam servitutem, a Deo quidem non abscidentem, in servitus autem iugo domantem eos, quemadmodum et Ezechiel propheta causas talis legis datae reddens ait..." Iraeneaus goes on to recall Stephen's speech (Acts 7:38-43) and, recalling also Exod. 32:2-3, underlines how such precepts have been given by God, even though through the mediation of an angel.

Jewish Carnality

reality, this, which recognizes different stages and must be subjected to an on-going, open-ended educational process, a reality that is formed through "many offerings" in divine service, which prepares the passage from "carnal things to spiritual things." Iraenaeus writes:

> He educated a people which was always ready to turn to the idols, training them to persevere in divine service, calling them through the secondary on to the principal things, that is through figures to truth, through temporal to eternal things, through carnal to spiritual things, through the earthly to the celestial [Iraenaeus here recalls how Moses received a vision of the celestial model of the tabernacle, and also recalls Paul, 1 Cor. 10:11.] "All these things, however, happened to them in figural form and they were written as a warning to us; through which the end of time was reached." Through the figures they learned to fear God and to persevere in his service.[78]

Here, we do not find only the figural value, nor is there any insensitivity toward the historical subjects. There certainly is, however, the sense of an accretive process *through* the history of the historical subjects. In insisting on the "through...to" construction there is the idea of a development which also passes through a stage of necessary error, the apparent deviation, the transgression, that pedagogic intervention uses to the general advantage of a humanity on its way to redemption.[79] The most evident demonstration of this positive evaluation of the regime of the law lies in the fact that *into the Church* itself are admitted precepts which accommodate the stubbornness of the people.[80] There is, in this attention to history, to materiality, to the body, the foundation of a theological anthropology of which it is difficult to find clear and more significant evidence elsewhere, even if in Clement of Alexandria we find analogous threads

---

[78] Adv. haer. IV 14, 3 (SC 100, 546): "Facilem ad idola reverti populum praestruens eos perseverare et servire Deo, per ea quae erant secunda ad prima vocans, hoc est per typica ad vera et per temporalia ad aeterna et per carnalia ad spiritalia et per terrena ad caelestia." This is a text which preceeds and gives fuller sense to the subsequent text, which I have cited already in the previous note. On this passage see Simonetti (1981). We can compare this stance with the more moderate one of Thomas' letter to Flora: dealing with the precepts given to those of a hard heart (especially divorce), it states that such a law is not divine but is a "second law" given as the lesser evil and different from the pure and simple law of God which was written on the tablets. It is this second law which permits the killing of those who kill, whereas the first had forbidden any type of killing (Ep. ad Flor. 4-5; SC 24,50-63).

[79] Adv. haer. IV 14,3 (SC 100, 548): "Per typos ergo discebant timere Deum et perseverare in obsequiis eius."

[80] The ancient Latin title of the paragraph puts this into sharp focus: "Quemadmodum in populo priore et in Ecclesia quaedem praecepta propter duritiam et indictoaudientiam data sunt" (SC 100, 368).

and the idea of accommodation.[81] The pedagogical function of the law is, furthermore, a New Testament idea (Gal. 3:24) and the theme will, of course, often appear in the subsequent development of Christian reflection.

Nevertheless, in the authors of the the fourth and fifth centuries the theme reappears accompanied by a nuanced scorn for a puerile/servile condition that the church no longer feels is an integral part of its own experience. It seems to me that this is the tone of the scornful words which Augustine reserves for the African Jews' "servile" observation of the sabbath and the manifestations of joy that accompany them. It is in the same way, I think, that the harsh indictment of Jewish carnality, which demands visible and material rewards in order to comply with the precepts and abstain from the idolatrous cult, should be interpreted. Once again the event of the golden calf serves as a lesson.[82] Even Cyril of Alexandria considers the

---

[81] See for example Paed. I 11 (GCS 12, 147): "In ancient times, the Logos taught through Moses, then through the prophets. But Moses was also a prophet, so that the law is education of children who are difficult to restrain. He says: 'Bloated, they rose to make revelry.' He says 'bloated,' not 'after eating,' to indicate the excess of food. And after they had indulged in excessive food, they exceeded in their revelry. For this reason the law came to them and with it the fear in order to distance themselves from sins and to exhort them to justice, preparing them to hear correctly the good teacher, that is to obey them: this is the same Logos that adapts itself according to need."

[82] See In Io. III 19 (CC 36, 29): "'Observa diem sabbati,' magis nobis praecipitur: quia spiritaliter observandum praecipitur. Iudaei enim serviliter observant diem sabbati, ad luxuriam, ad ebrietatem. Quanto melius feminae eorum lanam facerent, quam illo die in meanianis saltarent? Absit, fratres, ut illos dicamus observare sabbatum. Spiritaliter observat sabbatum christianus, abstinens se ab opere servili. Quid est enim ab opere servili? A peccato. Et unde probamus? Dominum interroga: 'Omnis qui facit peccatum, servus est peccati.' Ergo et nobis praecipitur spiritaliter observatio sabbati. Iam illa omnia praecepta nobis magis praecipiuntur, et observanda sunt: 'Non occides, non moechaberis, non furaberis, non falsum testimonium dices, honora patrem et matrem, non concupisces rem proximi tui, non concupisces uxorem proximi tui.' Nonne ista omnia et nobis praecipiuntur? Sed quaere mercedem, et invenies ibi dici: 'Ut expellantur hostes a facie tua, et accipiatis terram quam promisit Deus patribus vestris.' Quia non poterant capere invisibilia, per visibilia tenebantur. Quare tenebantur? Ne penitus interirent, et ad idola laberentur. Nam fecerunt hoc, fratres mei, sicut legitur, obliti tanta miracula quae fecit Deus coram oculis eorum. Mare discissum est; via facta est in mediis fluctibus; sequentes hostes eorum eisdem aquis operti sunt, per quas illi transierunt. Et cum Moyses homo Dei recessiset ab oculis eorum, idolum petierunt, et dixerunt: 'Fac nobis deos qui nos praeeant, quia ille homo dimisit nos.' Tota spes eorum in homine posita erat non in Deo. Ecce mortuus est homo; numquid mortuus est Deus, qui eruerat eos de terra Aegypti? Et cum fecissent sibi imaginem vituli, adoraverunt, et dixerunt: 'Hi sunt dii tui, Israel,

idea of divine pedagogy in the same vein, but so taken is he with his own invective that he denies the Jews "that shadow of future good" which, according to Paul (Heb. 10:1), comes from the observation of the law: by breaking the tablets, Moses deems them "worthy neither of the 'shade,' nor the 'figure,' nor even of divine pedagogy," "while those things were figures of what would happen to us in Christ."[83] We return here to the basic initial point of view, that of the pseudo-Barnabas, who removes any weight, relevance, effective history from the law and confers on it a singularly prospective sense, in relation to eschatology. The second tablets, God's accommodation to the needs of the people, the vicissitudes internal to the first pact are not even considered. This, in fact, was the position of Barnabas' Epistle, made keener, however, by Origen's writings, which had now been fully diffused and assimilated.

In turning now to Origen's exegesis, we may note how, not by chance, it appears superficial and hazy when dealing with the episode of the apostasy and, above all, the reiteration of the tablets. The episode is used here in a basically allegorical sense. The gift of the law is not received in the historical succession of the two different phases; the breaking of the tablets simply prefigures the end of the ancient testament: "Moses broke and threw away the first tablets of the law in the letter: he received the second law in the spirit and the second things are more stable than the first."[84] The historical truth, the historical *deuterosis* is not this, as we know. However, neither the point of view of the historical accommodation, nor that of the repression interest Origen much. Nor does he concern himself, as does Barnabas, with polemicizing directly with the Jews in order to deny that they ever effectively received the covenant. Rather, he is concerned to re-evaluate, from a spiritual point of view, the event that takes place at the foot of Mt. Sinai. The price he pays is the undoubted degeneration of the historical sense. The breaking of the tablets, in fact, signifies that degeneration:

> Let us return to Moses and we shall see how he values the letter of the law: he who, when he received the tablets of stone written by the finger of God, so honoured the letter of the law that he threw away the tablets he had in his hand, and broke them into pieces, the very tablets that had been written by the finger of God: yet, this is not

---

qui te liberaverunt de terra Aegypti.' Quam cito obliti tam manifestam gratiam! Quibus ergo modis teneretur populus talis, nisi promissis carnalibus?"
[83]De ador. Sp. et ver. I (PG 68, 144). See also C. Iul. IX (PG 76, 995-96), with a citation from Ezek. 20: 21-22.
[84]In Gen. hom. 9,1 (GCS 29, 88): "Primas tabulas legis in littera confregit Moyses et abiecit; secundam legem in spiritu suscepit et sunt firmiora secunda quam prima."

ascribed to him as a sin. You see then that it is not only Paul who scorns the letter of the law: long before him Moses scorned, threw away and broke the letter of the law, no doubt even then meaning that the honor and the worth of the law lay not in the letter but in the spirit.[85]

According to Origen, then, insofar as Moses' gesture of breaking the tablets, even though they have been written by the hand of God, is met by no admonition, it anticipates Paul's position on the letter of the law. Here, the dramatic and the concrete nature of the events as they happen is lost; they are used to signify something else. The long and troubled process of the covenant's promulgation is contracted into an overly rapid synthesis. The result is neither significant nor satisfying.

Evidently, interest in the historical event had now waned. Indeed, the burning questions at the end of the second century — for Iraenaeus and Justin the relationship with rabbinic Judaism, the gnostic devaluation of Old Testament materiality — were resolved in different and idiosyncratic ways on the basis of a spiritual synthesis. Thus, on the particular question of the reiteration of the tablets, Origen's solution proved decisive for the history of Christian interpretation, despite its glossing over of the historical dimension.

Origen's solution appears in the East from Gregory of Nyssa to George Caedrenus, a late Byzantine chronographer:[86]

> The first tablets [he says] are figures (*typos*) of the first law, according to the letter, as the second ones ... were figures of the second law, according to the Spirit. In the same way, the first people, who made the calf, represented figurally the first Israel, which was however lost in the wrath of God, together with the ancient law. But the second people represent the new Israel, according to Christ, who received and venerated the second tablets in the glory of the face of Moses.[87]

A similar reading appears in Severus of Antioch (sixth century). After narrating the story of Exod. 32, he comments:

---

[85]In Rom. II (PG 14, 917): "Revertamur ad ipsum Moysem, et videamus ipse quam magni fecerit litteram legis; qui cum accepisset tabulas lapideas inscriptas digito Dei, tantum honoris detulit litterae legis, ut proiceret de manibus suis tabulas, et comminueret quidem digito Dei scriptas, nec tamen hoc impietatis culpa notatus sit. Videas ergo quia non solus Paulus spernit litteram legis, sed multo ante eum Moyses et sprevit et abiecit et contrivit litteras legis, hoc sine dubio iam tunc designans, quod honor et virtus legis non esset in litteris, sed in spiritu."

[86]Nyssa, De vita Mosis II 216-17 (SC 1bis, 101-02).

[87]Hist. compend. 136 (PG 121, 167).

> This word [the command of Exod. 34:1 to go back to the mountain to receive the second tablets] shows with a symbol ... that when God had created man at the beginning and later recreated him with the new baptism of the child, he wrote on the tablets of his heart, which were pure, and which he had created and then renewed, his laws, firstly, the natural law and at the end the spiritual and evangelical law.[88]

And in the West, Augustine takes an analogous stance when he synthetically comments on the breaking of the tablets. He writes: "With a great mystery was figured the repetition of the pact, because the old one had to be abolished and the new had to be made."[89] Origen's approach thus passes into the history of interpretation; it carries at a given moment more or fewer original variations,[90] but it is transmitted in these exact terms by way of the *Glossa ordinaria* into the modern age.[91] From this standpoint, Augustine (and Origen with him) marks the age, and represents a watershed. In the next chapter, I shall attempt to show how, in concrete terms, the Origenian and Augustinian exegetic principle works. I will trace how not only the *iteratio testamenti* is identified in the historical episode of the golden calf, but how, also, figures and warnings, which are turned to Christian life in the present, are glimpsed in the particulars of the episode.

---

[88]Hom. 56 (PO 4, 75).
[89]Quaest. Exod. 144 (CC 33, 136): "Magno ... mysterio figurata est iteratio testamenti, quoniam vetus fuerat abolendum et constituendum novum."
[90]I would like here to note the work of Rabanus Maurus. He takes up the Augustinian stance but adds the necessary consideration that the second tablets, differently from the first ones, were written by Moses: an expression, this, of New Testament synergism between grace and human labor: "In secundis tabulis homo legitur scripsisse verba Dei, quia homo potest facere opus legis per caritatem iustitiae, quod non potest per timorem poenae" (En. Deut. 1, 15; PL 108, 872). Peter Damian: the second tablets will not be broken "quia Novi Testamenti gratia, quae crucis est solidata mysterium, nullum novit habere defectum" (Serm. 18; PL 144, 606). I have already referred to Gerhoh's text, according to which the destruction of the calf, *corpus diaboli*, literal sense, takes place on account of prayer.
[91]PL 113, 287. See the Additio V in Nicholas of Lyra, *ad loc.*, which notes that the *fractio* of the tablets cannot mean the *evacuatio* of the first law, which is irrepressible on account of its natural content, but its *traslatio* among the new people.

3

In the Church

1. Developments

The claim that Christian asceticism is born of prevalently Hellenistic influences is not easily proven. Against it stands not only the universality of ascetic and mystic instances, in the most varied of non-Christian religious contexts, but also, for example, the occurrence of non-Hellenistic Christianities (as in Syria where Christianity's monastic solution has the upper hand). In fact, the possibility of an asceticist evolution inhered in originary Christian experience. It was sufficient to transform the idea of a spiritual communion or conformity with Christ into a more or less materially minded project aimed at imitation, and this, indeed, is what happened.

The other side of the coin is that we find a people, often Christian only in name, supported by pastors from mainly monastic experiences who attempted to impose on the people a Christian form through the cult, institutions and above all a mode of preaching which displayed all its original defects. The ascetic and mystic sensibility returned in the pastoral practice as a series of substantially negative precepts presented in moralistic terms. The dossier of texts which revolves around the interpretation of the key passage (Exod. 32) – the primordial idolatrous fall – may serve to illustrate this development, insofar as it attributes to Moses a monastic and pastoral exemplarity, and views the tragic example of the fall in repressive terms.

There is also a second important element to this section: the degeneration of the debate on idolatry. Following on from a number of Paul's parenetic remarks,[1] idolatry is treated by analogy, transforming it into the equivalent of every form of over-estimation of worldly

---

[1] See Appendix I.2.

goods. This alternative lacks any understanding of the core of Jesus' protest and Paul's theological critique, both of which could be turned against any corruption of the monotheistic and anti-idolatrous commandment *within* the religious system itself. Luther's invective against false spirituality, which reveals its true carnality, and Calvin's psychological analysis of idolatry as the need for reassurance deserve, I believe, the greatest attention not only as important and fundamental intellectual breakthroughs, pertinent to any present reflection on religious experience, but also, as I have suggested for Luther, because they manifest the recovery of a genuinely biblical perception of the phenomenon of idolatry.

2. Moses, the Absentee

That the figure of Moses stands at the center in the vast chorus of interpretation results from interpreters' intuition. The gravity of his absence, it is unanimously noted, cannot be tolerated by the people – it is in the demand for a symbolic replacement for God but also for the mediator that the disastrous fall has its origin. Not surprisingly, then, for these interpreters, when Moses comes down the weight of his presence as intermediary and interceder is crucial in saving the situation. Philo describes him well. As the knower of men, Moses on the mountain understands what is happening down in the camp: "He knew ... that intoxication generates uncontrollable tumults, intemperance appeasement, and appeasement violence," *hybris*. Consequently, Moses is paralyzed by the conflict between "love of God" and "love of men," unable alone to bring the intimate conversation with God to an end, yet unable to accept that the people be crushed by the calamity of anarchy. Only the divine voice resolves the dilemma, rousing Moses first to offer the prayer of the "mediator and conciliator," and then to act rapidly and decisively, bringing the transgression to an end.[2]

It is hard not to recall this portrait when looking at how ancient authors describe the scene of the apostasy.[3] Of course, the pole around which the portrait is organized is the contrast between Moses and the people, between God's vision and idolatry, between mountain and plain, between *cor erectum* and *cor impinguatum*,[4] between destructive joy and expiatory condition,[5] between forty day fast and orgy,[6] between

---

[2]De vita Mosis, II 162-64 (Oeuvres 22, pp. 262-64).
[3]On the Christian Moses, see the contributions in Martin-Achard (1978).
[4]Tertullian (Ieiun. 6,5; CC 2, 1262), like many others after him, he sees in Moses the figure of Christ the mediator. See also Adv. Marc. II 26, 4 (CC 1, 505); Fug. 11, 1 (CC 2, 1148).
[5]See for example John Chrysostom, Ad Stagyr. III 3 (PG 47, 475).

In the Church

a pedagogue, immersed in the divine mystagogy – which participates in eternal life, cloaked in the cloud, as if "outside nature" – and the people who fall into disorder and licentiousness like children whose teacher is absent.[7] In sum: the contrast is expressed in the spatial terms of above and below:

> On the mountain, Moses struggled for you, down below you were moulding the calf; above he was pleading with God, below you provoked divine wrath and you worshipped the calf, you ate the manna and you insulted God.[8]
>
> On high, on the mountain, the law was given to Moses who was fasting: down below among the people who were eating, the sacrilegious prevarication was alight.[9]
>
> Moses fasts for forty days and forty nights on Mt. Sinai.... The satiated people make idols. He, without partaking of food, receives the law written by the finger of God. They, eating, drinking and rising to make revelry, mould the golden calf and prefer the Egyptian ox to the majesty of the Lord.[10]

Moses, like Mary, withdraws from worldy things, and so deserves to receive the law: Aaron, like Martha, agrees to practice a more worldly ministry, and thereby succumbs.[11]

3. "Continence is the Mother of Faith, Intoxication the Mother of Infidelity"

In the absence of their leader, the people jettison all restraint – the biblical account is very precise in establishing the exact order of events: the demand for symbolic replacements for Moses or God, liturgy, convivial celebration, orgiastic displays. Yet despite such clarity, subsequent commentators, especially Paul (but we must see what *epithymia-concupiscentia* really means for him), prefer to modify the order of events and establish a new link. Consider Jerome's perspective: Moses, *vacuo ventre*, receives the law; the appeased people give themselves over to idolatry. Indeed there is a tradition going back at least as far as Tertullian and Origen in which the ornaments on the ears and the reception of the word of God are connected – through a rather

---

[6]See again Chrysostom, In Gen. I hom. 1, 3 (PG 53, 24); see also Basil, De ieiun. hom. 1, 5 (PG 31, 169).
[7]Gregory of Nyssa, De vita Mosis I 58-59 (SC 1 bis, 25).
[8]Anastasius Sinaita, Disp. adv. iud. II (PG 89, 1235). See also Ephraem, Comm. ev. conc. VII 13 (SC 121, 146-47).
[9]Ambrose, De Helia et ieiun. 6, 16 (CSEL 32/2, 421); latin text cited above, ch.II, note 28.
[10]Jerome, Adv. Iov. II 15 (PL 23, 320).
[11]Peter Damian, De contemp. saec. 27 (PL 145, 280).

forced analogy. Here, giving up the ear-rings, as do the Israelites, is akin to giving up the divine word.[12] This odd analogy allows Origen to brand the foolish women with responsibility for the idolatry,[13] whereas the Jewish tradition attributes it exclusively to the men.[14] And this perspective can be traced in the East[15] and in the West[16] up to Luther ("verbum dei est ornatus aurium"),[17] who exploits it to underscore his constant message: idolatry lies in non-belief, not in lust.

Still it is the latter direction that most ancient exegesis takes: reprimands against vice, invitations to virtue. Thus we read in Ambrose, "Continence is the mother of faith, intoxication the mother of infidelity"[18] – a warning he gives both to the great people of the church, and to the small ranks of ascetes. While the resonances that recall Philo and Origen remain generic, with their invitation to beware of the sparkle of Egyptian wisdom[19] and to militate in the holy wars, following the example of the Levites who, rather than defect, serve as Moses' right hand men,[20] Tertullian's moralism by this stage has already firmly taken over the sequence: idolatry is the sister of fornication.[21] The edifying literature develops the link between incontinence (in food, drink, sex) and idolatry. Basil attacks the *gastrimarghia* (greed) which leads to the ruination of the people: whereas "fasting received the tablets written by the finger of God, intoxication broke them."[22] Why these emphases? The arrival in the Church of the masses must be addressed: a catechism to cover even the most elementary formative aspects is now needed.

The great pastor and rector of this time is, once again, John Chrysostom. It has already been noted that Chrysostom's approach to

---

[12]Scorp. 3, 3 (CC 2, 1074).
[13]In Exod.hom.13, 5(GCS 29, 277).
[14]The women refuse to give up their gold and the men, who also wear them according to the Arab fashion, give up theirs. See Ginzberg, *Legends*, vol. 3, p. 122, and vol. 6 note 265.
[15]For example, Basil, Comm. Isa. III 128 (PG 30, 325); Maximus Confessor, Quaest. Thalass. 16 (PG 90, 300), with an extremely elaborate psychological analysis which goes beyond the aims of the present work.
[16]Ambrose, Ep. 66 (PL 16, 1278) where a slightly different kind of symbolism emerges: *fidei signaculum*.
[17]Predigt uber das 2. Buch Mose 32 (WA 16, 622), of which more later.
[18]More precisely, the passage from Ambrose reads thus: "Videmus sacrilegium ebrietati fuisse coniunctum. Nam sicut mater fidei continentia est, ita perfidiae mater ebrietas est" (De Helai et ieiun. 12, 41; CSEL 32/2, 436).
[19]Origen, Ep. Gregor. 3(2) (SC 148, 190).
[20]Origen, In Num. hom. 3, 2 (GCS 30, 15-16). See De princ. IV 3, 12 (SC 268, 388).
[21]Scorp.3, 5(CC 2, 1075). See also Adv.Marc. II 18, 2 (CC 1, 495).
[22]De ieiun. 1, 5 (PG 31, 169).

Judaism, in terms of carnality, has little to do with Paul. Rather, it reflects greatly his concern, his pastoral zeal against the alluring Jewish feasts. Above all, it is the new year with its moments of penitential fasting and joy that disturbs him. To his eyes it appears both hypocritical and useless.[23] Yet setting aside these elements of his external polemic (in truth, it is said, his concern is primarily pastoral), the example of the people which "eats, drinks and revels" seems to him most opportune, all the more so because it is suggested by Paul. Thus, for Chrysostom, the cause of transgression, of idolatry, is *gastrimarghia*, which emerges as *paizein*, as revelry. He writes: "As they – says [Paul] – passed from the delights of idolatry, you too beware of falling."[24] And he draws on the numerous historical examples – not only the cases of Sodom, Noah and Esau, but even original sin itself depends on an alimentary transgression: "At the beginning death made its entrance on account of the excess in food." [25] The remark is interesting, but here it remains at a merely oratorial level and, as such, we find it again in various milieux, both Western and Eastern: "Greed precluded Paradise."[26]

By the fourth century monastic life has become luxurious. Ascetic reprimands, more or less addressed to a monastic public, draw on the calamitous experience of the Jewish people to invite the prodigals to continence or fasting. Exod. 32 is used to this end in the East, by Chrysostom.[27] Even earlier, Pachomius,[28] Basil,[29] and other masters of spiritual life similarly adopt it.[30] In the West, the memory of the

---

[23] This is the theme of the first sermon against the Jews (PG 48, 843 ff). In I Cor. hom. 23.3 (PG 61, 192).

[24] In I Cor. hom. 23.3 (PG 61, 192).

[25] In Gen. I hom. 1,2 (PG 53, 23). Other texts: In Matt. hom. 13,1 (PG 57, 209): Adam is thrown out of Paradise on account of intemperance; in I Cor. hom. 39, 9 (PG 61, 361); hom. I temp. Dom. 16 (PO 13, 124): "Adam died after having eaten and Israel died after the manna." See also Odo of Cluny, Coll. II 22 (PL 133, 567); Paschasius Radbertus, In Matt. III 4 (PL 120, 196); Peter of Poitier, Alleg. tab. Moysi 29 va (Moore and Corbett, p. 176). In Byzantine milieux only Gregory Palama is notable, Hom. 6, on fasting (PG 151, 85).

[26] Lotharius (Innocent III), De miser. hum. cond. 18 (Maccarrone, pp. 52 ff). An older text: Gregory the Great, Reg. past. III 19 (PL 77, 81).

[27] In Matt. hom. 55, 5 (PG 58, 545). See Palladius, De vita Io. Chrisost. 12 (Coleman and Norton, pp. 77 ff).

[28] S. Pachom. vita bohair. scr. 192 (CSCO 107, 118); see pseudo-Shenoute (CSCO 207, 35).

[29] See above n.22.

[30] Antiochus, De edac. hom. 4 (PG 89, 1444); Procopius of Gaza, Comm. Exod., *ad loc.* (PG 87/1, 663), corrected later in the *idolatria-vitia-carnis* sequence; Severian of Gabala, De mundi creat. or. 2,1 (PG 56, 429); John of Damascus,

events of Mt. Sinai is taken up by the Priscillianists[31] and, in the same rigorous sense, by Jerome in his *Adversus Iovinianum*.[32] Ambrose's aphorism, the title of the present section, "Continence is the Mother of Faith, Intoxication the Mother of Infidelity," summarizes an entire sensibility. Gregory the Great's *Regula pastoralis* authoritatively transmits the *edacitas-luxuria* sequence.[33] Likewise, Rabanus Maurus' *esus potusque-lusus-idolatria*.[34] The monastic school classifies and distinguishes, without separating them, the various degrees of *gastrimarghia*[35] and idolatry.[36] But Thomas Aquinas supplies a word of wisdom at the end of a *quaestio* in which he recalls the major sources (some of which are mentioned here). He concludes that the greed/idolatry link is neither absolute nor necessary.[37]

4. "Lusus"

I have put aside for a moment this particular aspect because seeing how it is reflected in the *ludere-paizein*, "playing" of the people ("they sat down to eat and drink and they rose to make revelry") may offer useful information. The Christians make little effort to grasp the historical and religious significance of the enthusiasm, the euphoria

---

Sacra par. 13, De ingluv. et gul. (PG 95 1332 ff); Philoxenus of Mabbug, Hom. 10, 403 (SC 44, 359-60); Martyrius (Sahdona), Lib. perf. II 7, 8 and 32 (CSCO 215, 76-77 and 84).
[31]Ep. Titi de dispos. sanctimon. (PLS 2, 1533).
[32]See above, n.10.
[33]Reg. past. III 19 (PL 77, 81): "Quos plerumque edacitas usque ad luxuriam pertrahit, quia, dum satietate venter extenditur, aculei libidinis excitantur. Unde et hosti callido, qui primi hominis sensum in concupiscentia pomi aperuit, sed in peccati laqueo strinxit, divina voce dicitur: 'Pectore et ventre repes [Gen. 3:14] ac si ei aperte diceretur: cogitatione et ingluvie super humana corda dominaberis. Quia gulae deditos luxuria sequitur, propheta testatur, qui dum aperta narrat, occulta enuntiat, dicens: "Princeps cocorum destruxit muros Ierusalem"' [Jer. 52, 14 LXX]." Eutropius Abbas, Ep. VIII vit. (PL 80, 11): eating at the wrong time, the superfluous, sophistications.
[34]Comm. Exod. IV 16 (PL 108, 222). See also, again by Rabanus, In Gal. 5 (PL 112, 354; see 357): "Qui enim se semel luxuriae voluptatique permiserit, non respicit Creatorem. Alias autem omni idolatria, festivitate, gula, ventre et his quae infra venter sunt, delectatur." See also Atto, I n I Cor. 10 (PL 134, 372); Rupert of Deutz, De s. Trin. 28, 5, 13 (CC cont. med. 24, 1991).
[35]Eutropius Abbas, Ep. VIII vit. (PL 80, 11): eating at the wrong time, the superfluous, sophistications.
[36]Alan of Lille, Serm. 2 (PL 210, 203): *baccilatria, nummilatria, carnilatria*.
[37]Quaest. disp., De malo, q.14, art.2, resp. ad 6: "Gula dispositive inducit ad idolatriam et luxuriam; non autem ita quod haec duo sint de ratione gulae; unde non sequitur quod peccatum gulae sit peccatum mortale; quia etiam peccatum veniale potest disponere ad mortale."

and the orgiastic explosion with which the revelry of the Israelites culminates. As previously in the Jewish tradition, we see here a basic allusion to sexual excesses: "Scripture would not have spoken of revelry if it had not been wanton," says Tertullian.[38] Yet, there is one standpoint which attributes to *lusus*, "play" a less drastic meaning: the fall to *mataia*, to vain, lazy, inane things, events which are extraneous or averse to a life dedicated to ultimate things.[39] Thus, while John Chrysostom grasps and inveighs against the feverish and vacuous excitation of the Jews at the foot of Mt. Sinai,[40] he also exploits the occasion to assault the lazy and invite them to work.[41] We must not dedicate our entire time to revelry, to feasts and banquets, to the theatre (important theme of the fathers), he advises, for "it is not God who gives *paizein*, but the devil" – as is proved by the example of the Israelites at the foot of Mt. Sinai, the fate of the inhabitants of Sodom and of those who watched while Noah laboured and even made fun of him; Noah did not joke, nor did God.[42]

Cyril of Alexandria's interpretation hinges decidedly on the sense of fornication (*porneia*). He recommends "fasting, imitation of angelic life, source of temperance, principle of continence, abolition of lasciviousness."[43] Ambrose too gives *lusus* a carnal meaning akin to sensuality and bestial instinctiveness, and draws the kind of conclusions he had previously drawn when discussing *ebrietas*: it is *lusus* which leads Jacob from the *fidei veritas* to the *perfidiae error*.[44] And Jerome, recalling both Exod. 32 and the episode of Noah's intoxication and nudity, concludes: "First the belly, then the rest."[45]

Gregory the Great insists on the "weak" sense of *lusus*, on the *mane gaudemus*, the *vitium* which is intimately connected to convivial *voluptas* (because *voluptas* can only be vice).[46] In his sermons, Gregory underlines that the passage from *edacitas*, "voracity," to *lusus* takes

---

[38] Ieiun. 6, 2 (CC 2, 1262): "lusus nisi impudicus non denotasset."
[39] The same verb *shq* permits this double sense: see Jerome, Hebr. quaest. Gen. 21, 9 (CC 72, 24). Didymus the Blind, Comm. Ps. 25, 4 (Gronewald, pp. 164 ff); Asterius the Sophist, In Ps. 11 hom. 3, 30 (Richard, p. 171).
[40] Exp. Ps. 4, 3 (PG 55, 43-44).
[41] Ad Stagyr. I 3 (PG 47, 429). Against sloth, with reference to Exod 32, see Nilus of Ancyra, Ep. 1, 310 (PG 79, 136); Mose bar Kefa, De Parad. I (PG 111, 576).
[42] In Matt. hom. 6, 6-7 (PG 57, 70-71).
[43] Hom. pasch. 1, 4 (PG 77, 413). Germanus of Costantinople, In dom. corp. sepolt. (PG 98, 272): the Jews, inebriated with fury, rise to make revelry against the Word.
[44] Expl. Ps. 38, 34 (CSEL 64, 209).
[45] Ep. 22, 8 (CSEL 54, 1 55).
[46] Mor. Iob I 8, 10 (CC 143, 29).

place through *loquacitas*, "loquacity."[47] In the comments of later interpreters, light touches and different nuances multiply. For example, Aimon of Halberstadt reads "many games, dances, fornication";[48] Bruno the Carthusian considers *lusus* "scorn" for divine gifts;[49] Rupert of Deutz declares: "They venerated the gods ... on account of their belly and genitals ... they abandoned themselves to a depraved *lusus*, the *lusus* of ignominy";[50] Godefridus calls it "the dissolution of the spirit."[51] Alan of Lille faces the question in a systematic manner, distinguishing between the meanings of *deludere, idolatrare* (Exod. 32), *auguriari, delectari*.[52] Hervaeus declares: "dancing ... or playing before the calf, that is worshipping the calf: to venerate idols is similar to a child's game."[53] Indeed, more than one commentator identifies puerile traits in *lusus* (the greek *paizein* helps). The *Glossa ordinaria* is clear: "To play, that is, to worship, which is similar to a child's game. Children are inclined to play. What is more like a child's game than making idols?"[54] To worship is a *fatuissimus lusus*.[55]

So unlike the Jewish rabbinic tradition, which recognizes immediately the orgiastic side of *lusus* ("the rabbis – explains Cornelius a Lapide – use *ludere* in a very basic sense, to mean fornicate"),[56] Christian interpretation hesitates between the harshness of Tertullian's old line ("the Scripture would not have spoken of play if it had not been wanton") and a certain literal-minded exegesis for which *lusus* indicates game, amusement, child's play,

---

[47]In ev. II hom. 40, 5 (PL 76, 1307): "Priusquam ad lusum moveatur corpus, ad iocos et verba inania movetur lingua." See also Aelred of Rielvaux, De inst. inclus. 7 (SC 76, 62): "Omne colloquium et dissolutionis materiam caveat."
[48]Aimon of Halberstadt, In I Cor. 10 (PL 117, 561).
[49]Bruno the Carthusian, In I Cor. 10 (PL 153, 174): "lusus et deisio."
[50]Rupert of Deutz, De s. Trin. 19, In Deut. 2, 7 (CC cont. med. 22, 1088).
[51]Godefridus, Hom. 76 (PL 174, 538).
[52]Dist. dict. theol., ludere (PL 210, 811).
[53]Hervaeus, In I Cor. 10 (PL 181, 911).
[54]Glossa ord. a 1 Cor. 10, 7 (PL 114, 535): "Ludere, id est adorare, quod ludo puerorum simile. Facile namque ad lusum est pueritia. Quid autem lusui puerili tam simile est quam idola facere?" Bonaventure, Comm. Sap. 15, 12 (ed. Quaracchi 6, 207): "Lusum esse etc. hoc dicit, quia idola facere et colere ludo puerorum videtur simile esse, et sic qui faciunt imagines luteas et adorant." Similarly, Bernardino of Siena, Dom. IX post Pent., post. (Opera 9, p. 216). See also Jan Hus, Serm. temp. 70 (Schmidtova, p. 395): "Ludere, id est instar puerorum adorare vitulum, sicut faciunt pueri de luto vitulum confingentes."
[55]Dionysius the Carthusian, En. Exod. 32, art. 62 (Opera 2, p. 98).
[56] Comm. Exod. (ed. cit., 578).

loquaciousness, dance. Yet this is not to trivialize the issue. Indeed, as the *Glossa ordinaria* suggests, it is to these apparently trivial things that we must pay most attention because the chain may lead on to ruination: "Eating and drinking incline you to play, play to idolatry: if the sin of vanity is not immediately repressed the unprepared mind is overcome by iniquity. Therefore: 'Whoever does not beware of small things, little by little, will fall.' If, in fact, inadvertently seduced, we neglect to pay attention to small things, we end up by committing more serious things."[57] The doctrine is strict: we must be vigilant about small and innocuous things because they habituate us to worse sins. Albert the Great's admonition is explicit: "Play is already incontinence, because as the Philosopher says, the playful man is incontinent" (the philosopher here is Aristotle, of course, but the reading is somewhat tendentious).[58] Thomas Aquinas is no less forthright: "he who exceeds in play commits a mortal sin,"[59] and even he who is unable to play (*ludere*) and prevents others from playing, is sinful. (This is, however, a minor defect ["it is a less serious sin, in play, a lack more by omission than by defect."].)[60]

All this "seriousness" – not so much that of Thomas, behind which can be glimpsed Hellenistic ideals, but that of Gregory, which makes *voluptas* the equivalent of sin – is unfamiliar to our contemporary ears. So we must examine more closely and in concrete terms where the pastor and the moralist locate *lusus*. To that end we must refer to the canonic and moral literature which, for the most part, stand outside the concerns of the present work. Even from the few sources available to us here (commentaries, treatises, sermons), we can glimpse something of that reality which theology and pastoral prudence aim to keep under control. Consider, for example, the *lusa diabolica*[61] in high-medieval literature; the *ludi inordinati* or *mundiales* of a magical character in Franciscan preaching (full of terrifying examples for the people);[62] the

---

[57] "Esus potusque ad lusum impulit, lusus ad idolatriam: quia si vanitatis culpa non caute compescitr, ab iniquitate mens incauta devoratur. Unde: 'Qui modica spernit, paulatim decidit.' Si enim cavere parva negligemus insensibiliter seducti, etiam maiora audenter perpetramus" (PL 114, 287).

[58] Post. Isa. 57, 9 (Opera 19, p. 544). The reference is to Eth. Nicom. VII 8, 1150 b 16. Referring to the Grossatesta version, Aristotle says: "Videtur autem et lusivus intemperatus esse, est autem mollis" (Arist. lat. 26, 1-3, 4, 508).

[59] Summa theol. II 2, q. 168, art. 3, resp.

[60] Ibid., art. 4, resp.

[61] Firminus Abbas, De sing. libr. canon. scarap. (PL 89, 1041).

[62] See *Liber exemplorum ad usum praedicatorum*, ed. Little (Aberdeen 1908), "De ludis inordinatis."

orgies among demons and witches,[63] and even gambling, the banal object of the most violent attack by preachers[64] insofar as it is the ruination of poor people ("mandant hominem ad hospitalem vel ad furcas"),[65] the direct cause of 42 sins and the invention of the devil.[66]

5. Ecclesial Applications

The unhappy experience of the Jewish people lent itself to pastoral moralizing, but since Moses and Aaron were also involved, between them carrying some of the responsibility, the pastors of the church could draw some further useful lessons. For instance, from his consideration of such a complex situation Gregory the Great suggests that the good shepherd treat his flock with both discipline and mercy.[67] By contrast, according to Bruno of Segni the complicated roles of Moses and Aaron show that the pastor must stand against the delights of the people and reproach their foolishness.[68] And for his part, Dionysius the Carthusian derives both a warning of the danger – the gravest danger, as he sees it – which could follow from the absence of the pastor, and a sign of the responsibility of his possible vicar.[69] In the age of the Counter Reformation, these admonitions were to become all the more insistent.[70]

The "anarchy" of the people is sometimes seen, in contrast to the absence of the pastor, as a kind of ethical subversiveness. Consider Cyprian's *De bono patientiae*, which innovates the model of Tertullian's *De patientia*. Cyprian writes: "impatience, even in the church, creates heretics and, like the Jews, leads to hostile hatred and

---

[63]Alphonsus de Castro, Opusc. sortileg. et malefic. haeresi (in "Malleus maleficarum," Lyon 1669, vol. 2, t.2, p. 212): "Daemon ille, qui in solio maiestatis sedet, praecepit omnibus ut tripudient, et psallent cum gaudio et laetitia sumentes voluptates suas. Et unusquisque daemon manu apprehendit mulierum suam, ad cuius custodiam deputatus erat, et cum illa saltat, et choreas facit: choreis et salationibus finitis inde ad mensas veniunt, quae lautissimus ferculis ornatae et praeparatae inveniuntur, ut quisquis ad libitum illis vescatur. Conviviis expletis luminaria extinguuntur omnia, et quisque daemon in forma incubi suam capit mulierem."
[64]Giacomo della Marca, Serm. 10, De ludo (Sermones dominicales, ed. R. Lioi, vol. 1, pp. 190-205).
[65]Ibid., p. 192.
[66]Ibid., pp. 195-202.
[67]Reg. past. II 6 (PL 77, 38).
[68]Exp. Exod. *ad. loc.* (PL 164, 367).
[69]En. Exod. 32, art. 63 (Opera 2, pp. 106 ff).
[70]John of Avila, Serm. 12 and 35 (Obras completas, Madrid 1953, vol. 2, pp. 517 and 1257).

In the Church 65

furious rebellions against the peace and charity of Christ."[71] This theme was also to appear later: the *sermo haereticus* is the golden calf, externally beautiful, but internally empty and meaningless.[72] Such applications correspond to the notion of the just divine punishment which strikes subversives and deviants.

Here a long chapter in interpretation opens. The theme of the repression of the heretics, taking Exod. 32 as its starting point, runs from Augustine to Calvin through Thomas Aquinas. Over time it has been studied in all its fundamental aspects.[73] Christianity thus absorbs the lesson that Moses had so rigorously taught.

For instance, to those who object: "Why is it written in the law 'You shall not kill, he who kills his neighbour will die a death,' and they, killing their brothers, receive praise and blessing?" Hippolytus answers, "It is one thing to kill a sinful man, another to kill a righteous man: we must distinguish between murder and murder."[74] The intransigence of Moses, *vir mitissimus*, is admired. Moreover, do not the words of Jesus – "I came to bring the sword" – echo the revenge of the sons of Levi on the multitude who betrayed?[75]

6. Idolatry and Monotheism

The analysis of idolatry carried out by ancient Christian authors is disappointing. When the confession of faith of the martyrs concludes, when Origen's anti-pagan polemic, of which the greatest model is the polemic against Celsus, ceases to be relevant (as was already the case in the fourth century, with the exception of the episode involving

---

[71] Bon. pat. 19 (CC 3, 129): "Impatientia etiam in Ecclesia haereticos facit et, ad iudaeorum similitudinem, contra Christi pacem et caritatem rebelles ad hostilia et furiosa odia compellit."

[72] Rupert of Deutz, De s. Trin. 26, In Reg. 5, 6 (CC cont. med. 22, 1413); Haimo of Halberstadt, En. Os. 11 (PL 117, 86); Gerhoh of Reichersberg, Comm. Ps. 105, 23 (PL 194, 655); Hildegard of Bingen, Scivias II, vis. 7, 23 (CC cont. med. 43, 322).

[73] See Walzer (1968), p.14. Walzer refers mainly to Augustine, Ep. 93, 6; Thomas Aquinas, Summa theol. II 2, q.64, artt. 3 and 4; Calvin, Instit. IV 20, 10 and various other texts. To this dossier could be added: Lucifer of Cagliari, De non parc. in Deo delinquent. 1 (CSEL 14, 209 ff); Gregory the Great, Reg. past. III 25 (PL 77, 97); Rabanus Maurus, Comm. Exod. IV 16 (PL 108, 221 ff), purely descriptive; some very decisive affirmations by Peter Damian: Lib. gomor. 25 (PL 145, 189): spiritual war, in Origen's sense, as also in Serm. 3 (PL 144, 519); Opusc. 57, De princ. off. coercit. improb. 3 (PL 145, 322); Richard of St-Victor, Beniam. min. 40 (PL 190, 30) in a spiritual sense; Hus, Serm. 70 (Schmidtova, p. 337): prohibit at least the excesses, if not to pass directly to the sword.

[74] Ben. Mos. 2 (PO 27, 157).

[75] See John Chrysostom, In Matt. hom. 35, 1 (PG 57, 406).

Julian and the reaction it provoked among Christian intellectuals),[76] in-depth research into the essence of the so-called idolatrous phenomenon also ceases. The biblical arguments, to which I have referred, also seem to fall away into repetitions lacking any link to personal experience. It almost seems that the two commandments – you will have no other God, and do not make images – touch all but Christians; idolatry is always the sin of others.

This is not the place for an exhaustive demonstration. Yet even the most modest of itineraries such as the one I am here following, which is tied to the specific memory of one biblical episode, the golden calf, cannot fail to confirm this direction. In this case, we encounter for evidence a sustained and overly rhetorical invective against *anoia*, *mania*, ignorance, the madness of worshipping animals.[77] Along Origen's lines, and in scholastic language, the difference between simulacrum (reproduction of beings existing in nature) and idol[78] is explained (or what *eidos-latria* means).[79] The difference between idolatry *opinione* and idolatry *moribus*, or between idolatrous theory and practice, as we might put it today, is elaborated.[80] Attempts are made to bring the idolatrous commandment up-to-date with translated and metaphorical reworkings ("God, for each one of us, is what we honour above all else, what we admire and love above all").[81] This is a generic use of the notion that is found in Paul, where the apostle identifies idolatry and avarice (Eph. 5:6; Col. 3:5),[82] with who knows how many precedents, even among non-Christian moralists.

Even the *Glossa ordinaria* passes on this notion when, debating the (correct) problem of the plural "make us gods to walk before us," it explains that the calf "was one only, in the likeness of Apis, but is spoken of in the plural because with idolatry one is subject to a

---

[76]I am thinking of Contra Iulianum by Cyril of Alexandria (IV 149; PG 76, 729), which carries out a bitter polemic, based on Exod. 32, against the intermediary beings (where God works directly on his people).

[77]Theodoretus of Cyrrhus, In Ps. 105, 19-20 (PG 80, 1725-26); see also John Chrysostom, In Act. Ap. hom. 7,2 (PG 60,1 36).

[78]Origen, In Exod. hom. 8, 3 (GCS 29, 221-22); fragment in Exod. 20, 4 (PG 17, 16); Theodoretus of Cyrrhus, Quaest. Exod. 38 (PG 80, 264); Procopius of Gaza, Comm. Exod. 20, 3 (PG 87/1, 606); Rabanus Maurus, Comm. Exod. II 12 (PL 108, 95).

[79]Haimo of Halberstadt, In I Cor. 11 (PL 117, 560-61).

[80]Radulphus, Hom. II 20 (PL 155, 2013).

[81]Radulphus, Hom. II 20 (PL 155, 2013).

[82]See Radulphus, Hom. I 39 (PL 155, 1804); Bruno the Carthusian, In Eph., *ad. loc.* and In Col., *ad. loc.* (PL 153, 343 and 391).

multitude of vices."[83] This kind of moralism is found up to Erasmus: to worship idols is an easy option because idols permit any debauchery, any disorder, whereas the real God would prevent it.[84]

Only with the Reformation does the theme of idolatry, like many of the others on which I have dwelt, regain its vitality. The episode of the golden calf leaves its place in the repertory of "examples" to become (once again) a crucial discussion point in biblical history, especially for Luther.

Luther is led to meditate on the theme by his interpretation of Psalm 105. In dealing with verses 19-23 in the *Dictata super psalterium* (1513-1516), he expresses his awareness not only of a deep ecclesiastic crisis but also of his own growing role, a role which is likened, it would seem, to that of Moses. First, "transform our own glory into the likeness of a calf which eats hay" finds a mystical interpretation: the glory is the faith, transformed into carnal wisdom. Second, the calf, in the vision of Ezekiel and in the usage of Paul, (1 Cor. 9:9), stands for preaching, which must feed on spiritual manna and not be held back. Third, Moses stands between God and the people at the moment of the fracture *(fractio)*; that fracture foretells the greater split between the Church and Israel at the time of Christ on account of the latter's unbelief. It also prefigures the fracture before Luther's eyes in his contemporary world, but which lacks any Moses. Luther writes: "And today there is a painful fracture *(confractio)* because there is no Moses to mediate, because his law is dead."[85]

---

[83]PL 113, 286: "...deos pluraliter cum unus tantum vitulus factus sit ad similitudinem scilicet bovis Apis, quem in Aegypto coluerunt, sed qui idolatriam colit, omnibus vitiis subiicit se, et quasi tot diis et daemonibus quot vitiis servit." See also Jerome, In Dan. I 3, 14b (CC 75A, 800): "Alii hanc dicunt Scripturae consuetudinem ut unum idolum appellet pluraliter." At least from Augustine on, it is deemed normal that the plural in Scripture can exist alongside the singular: see Enchir. XIII 44 (CC 46, 74), taken up again since Peter Lombard, Sent. II, dist. 33, cap. 2 (ed. Quaracchi 2, 483). Chrysostom: in any case it was polytheism (De poenit. hom. 7, 5 ; PG 49, 330). Or else: they spoke in the plural because they were drunk (In Act. Ap. hom. 7, 2; PG 60, 136).

[84]Lingua 446-50 (Opera 4/1, 305-06): "Gentes daemonia malunt colere quam verum Deum, quod hic detestatur omnem turpitudinem, illi favent vitiis et alunt pravas cupiditates, nec offenduntur, cum in ludis ac fabulis tales inducuntur, qualem nemo vir bonus vellet esse suum filium, aut uxorem, atque adeo ne famulum quidem."

[85]WA 44, 200: "'Si non Moses electus eius' i.e., prae ceteris gratissimus 'stetisset' intercedendo 'in confractione' i.e., plaga, qua erant confringendi et disperdendi." See ibid. the gloss to "stetisset": "Hebr. 'stetisset medius contra faciem illius.' Unde metaphoram nostra translatio [the Vulgate] servat, quando enim res frangitur, media dividitur. Sic in medio et fractione esse idem est. Ita populus et Deus divisi iam erant, sed inter partes divisas mediat Moses:

When Luther again takes up this theme in 1525, the break has already been made. The same procedure with which the Baal, the Astaroth, the Dagon and so on were erected, has led to the creation of idols of saints like Benedict, Francis, and the Pope, because "we think we please God with rites and doctrines" (here Paul's argument, "having known God, they did not glorify him as God" is relevant).[86] Annotating Deut. 4:2 ("Your eyes have seen"), he observes that more recent idolaters have not venerated demons as demons, but believed they were serving the true God no less than did the Jews when they fell into the sin of idolatry, no less than did even the most holy and religious papists.[87]

Idolatry, then, keeps the name of the true God but attributes to God its own contrivances ("retento nomine veri Dei sine vera cognitione dei"). A little later in the same text, Luther refutes a banal interpretation of idolatry as surrender to sexuality.[88] These are themes that he was to take up on many occasions. For instance, on December 16th 1526 (the third Sunday of Advent), taking Exodus as his text he points to Aaron's terrible responsibilities.[89] And the next Sunday, the fourth Sunday of Advent, he returns to the theme. He declares (1) that heresy is born of boredom with the word of God, and (2) from ingratitude comes the preaching which betrays the word: "The beginning of every heresy is ingratitude and tedium with the word ... Aaron is here at his worst ... After the ingratitude, then, the calf is certain to follow, in other words, the new preaching which ignores the

---

tamen ad Deum versus 'in cospectu inquit eius.' Per istam autem confractionem a longe preludit ad eam, quae facta est tempore Christi, de qua Rom. XI 'rami fracti sunt, ut ego inserar' [11:19]. Et iterum: 'fracti sunt propter incredulitatem [11:20]. Ne ergo tunc ita simul in unum omnes confringerentur, Moses se interposuit, sed quod tunc minatus fuit, nunc tandem implevit. Et est hodie miserrima confractio, quia nullus nunc Moses mediat, quia est mortua lex eius." We must compare with Augustine, En. Ps. 105,21 (CC 440, 1562); "Ubi demonstratum est intercessio sanctorum quantum pro aliis valeat apud Deum. Securus enim Moyses de iustitia Dei, qua eum delere non posset, impetravit misericordiam, ne illis quos iuste posset, deleret."
[86]Ibid., 588: "Omnibus illis ritibus et doctrinis opinamur nos Deo placere."
[87]Deut. Mosi cum annot. 44,3 (WA 14, 587): "Moabitae et aliae gentes non coluerunt daemonia, quod scirent esse daemonia, sed crediderunt sese Deo vero servire non minus quam iudaei idolatrae, imo quam omnes nostri papistae etiam sanctissimi et religiosissimi."
[88]Ibid., 589: "Multi putant Priapum fuisse."
[89]WA 16, 614R: "Horrendissimum est, quod Aaron electus, vocatus a Deo sacerdos, cadit in peccatum."

word of God."[90] To make gods, explains Luther, means to take over the name and the word of God with our own thoughts.[91] A harsh indictment of the factious, and the interpretation of *tantzen* (dances) as a fatuous glorification of piety ensues: "They are dancers and acrobats, that is people who seek their own honour and glory."[92] The same themes reappear after Christmas in the sermon given Sunday 30th December 1526. Here, however, the emphasis is switched to Aaron. From his example, Luther deduces that being instructed in the Scriptures and the recipient of benefits and miracles does not guarantee one from being abandoned by God.[93] Aaron's tragic case enables Luther to draw powerfully the image of stubbornness, the real sin against the spirit, because it is an "inversion" of the word of God and profanation of his honor.[94]

In a comment made some years later on Paul's Letter to the Galatians (4:8), Luther insists on the idolatrous experience as a subjective fiction tied to a perverse use of reason: it is from the "Deus est" of natural reason that conditions fertile for idolatry are born.[95]

---

[90]WA 619 BR: "Initium omnis haeresis est ingratitudo et taedium verbi ... Aaron hic est pessimus ...post ingratitudinem itaque certissime semper sequitur vitulus, i.e., nova praedicatio quae ignorat verbum Dei."

[91]Ibid., 620R and BR: "Vide in Scriptura, quid sit Deum facere, ist so viel, dass ich sein Namen, Wort nehme und deuts et lenks [I explain and lead] sicut volo ... Deum facere, ut hic vides, est nomen Dei accipere verum eiusque verbum et opus illud appropriare nostris cogitationibus. Sic enim faciunt. Accipiunt illud opus veri Dei: 'Eduxit ex Aegypto,' et nomen Dei, et tribuunt illud secundum cor suum vitulo. Ita fit et in aliis. Monachus cogitat remissionem peccatorum, gratiam Dei etc. quae vera sunt et naturalia opera Dei, sed tribuit ea suis observationibus: si sic vestio, edo, ieiuno etc. remittuntur peccata, cumulo meritum, placet maxime Deo."

[92]Ibid., 625BR: "Post istam devotionem sequitur securitas et animus iucundus et crapula, quia placent omnia, laudantur, omnia promovent saltationem inter papistas, non est ibi crux et displicentia priorum operum, gaudent de inventu novo cultu, qui, si cultus dei esset, negligeretur egregie."

[93]Ibid., 627BR: "Ut iam nemo sit securus [there is here an echo of the *Dies irae*], quod sit miraculis et benefitiis honoratus, quod doctus in Scripturis et ideo senserat: securus ero, non me deseret."

[94]Ibid., 628R.

[95]WA 40/1, 608 Dr: "Hoc Paulus significat, cum ait: 'cum ignorabatis Deum,' id est cum nesciebatis, quae esset voluntas Dei, 'serviebatis iis, qui natura dii non erant,' id est, serviebatis somniis et cogitationibus cordis vestri, quibus fingebatis Deum hoc vel illo opere seu ritu colendum esse. Nam hinc, quod homines tenuerunt hanc maiorem [the major premiss of the syllogism]: 'Deus est,' nata est omnis idolatria, quae sine cognitione divinitatis ignota fuisset in mundo. Quia vero homines hanc naturalem cognitionem de Deo habebant, conceperunt extra et contra verbum vanas et impias de Deo cogitationes, quas

What follows is an all-out attack on religious orders and their religiosity. He declares that the flesh of which Paul speaks (Gal. 5:20) has nothing to do with sexuality taken in a narrow sense, as we have seen. Indeed, it is those very monks, closed up in their cells, who claim to have reached the highest peaks of spiritual experience, that yield to the flesh, swamped by the presumption of their own justice and piety:

> The highest point of religiosity, of holiness and burning pity [*religio*, with various nuances] of those who render homage to God without the word or the blessing of God, is idolatry. This happened under the papacy, when it was held to be a most spiritual thing that the monks in the cells meditated on God and his works. Inflamed by burning devotion, they bent their knees, prayed and contemplated celestial things with such delight as to cry for the over-arching joy. Here was not thought of woman or other creature, but only of the Creator and his miraculous works. And yet, this most spiritual thing is clearly, according to Paul, work of the flesh. For this reason, every form of religiosity, with which homage is rendered to God without his word and his commandment, is idolatry.[96]

How so? The Pauline notion of flesh is far wider than the "papist" commentators would admit. It does not include only and exclusively sexual practice, rather it stretches to touch on religious presumption – above all that of the monastic orders under the Pope.

Luther's conviction here goes back to his first commentary on the Letter to the Galatians (1519), where, *contra* Jerome (who in turn had followed Origen), he affirmed that he was not willing at any price to "separate flesh, soul, spirit." Now, a decade later, his thought is crystallized, his polemic sharper. He concludes:

> But this above all must be remarked, how the papists have so obscured the meaning of the word flesh that they collapse the work of the flesh in coitus and satisfaction of desire. But here [Gal. 5:20] the work of the flesh is idolatry, highest good and wisdom for men, like the

---

amplexi sunt tanquam ipsam veritatem illisque Deum finxerunt aliter quam natura est."

[96] WA 40/2, 110 Hs: "Summae religiones, sanctitates er ardentissimae religiones eorum, qui sine verbo et mandato Dei colunt Deum, sunt idolatria. Ut in papatu habebatur pro actu spiritualissimo, quando monachi sedentes in cellis meditabantur de Deo et eius operibus, quando inflammati ardentissimis devotionibus genu flectebant, orabant et coelestia contemplabantur, tanta delectatione, ut prae nimio gaudio lachrymarentur. Ibi nulla erat cogitatio de mulieribus aut de creatura alia, sed tantum de Creatore et eius mirabilibus operibus. Et tamen ista spiritualissima res, ut ratio iudicat, est iuxta Paulum opus carnis. Quare omnis talis religio, qua colitur Deus sine verbo et mandato eius, idolatria est." See also Tischr. 6584 (WA 6, 56).

In the Church

Pope who, with the monks and the priests, instituted religious orders, which seem today the most spiritual.[97]

And ten years later, in a sermon given on August 10, 1544 on I Corinthians, Luther reinforces his stance. Once again, at the center of his analysis stand the broadening of the concept of the work of the flesh and the denunciation of religious presumption as the essence of idolatry.[98] As I have noted, these are the typical themes of Luther's anti-idolatrous considerations. Yet not by chance, a year before he had published the violent pamphlet *On the Jews and their Lies*. And the sermon brings a new tendency to light and marks an involution of Luther's thought. Now he escalates his polemic against the Jews. In a maneuver that impoverishes the analysis and achievements of preceding years, Luther aims at an external target, Judaism, the same critique that previously and with pitiless lucidity he had turned on Christianity.[99]

In the same year (1541), Calvin gives form to his interpretation of the capital and idolatrous experience narrated in Exod. 32 (*Institution chretienne*). In the dedicatory letter, Calvin too dwells on Aaron's responsibilities and on his fallibility despite his position as consecrated priest.[100] Calvin's comment, powerfully centered on the theme of "pride and awe,"[101] underlines the psychological aspects of a procedure which brings the man who does not believe in the invisible proximity of God to invent a "mask or phantasm which answers his madness."[102] The comment on Exodus, as in that on the mysterious

---

[97]WA 40/2, 111 Hs ff: "Hoc insigniter notandum, quia vocabulum carnis apud papistas sic obscuratum, ut opera carnis dicantur concubitum et libido expleta. Sed hic opera carnis idolatria, id summum et maxima sapientia in homine, ut papa cum monachatu et Pfaffen instituit religiones, quae videntur spiritualissimae." For the brief commentary to St. Paul's Letter to the Galatians (1519), referred to in the text, see WA 2,585: "Ego mea temeritate carnem, animam, spiritum prorsum non separo."
[98]WA 49, 540-41.
[99]Von den Juden und ihren Lügen, 1543; for idolatry, see in particular WA 53, 436-37.
[100]Inst. relig. chrest. Ep. au Roy, ed. Benoit (Paris 1957) vol. 1, p. 43. It is said that the catholics defended themselves from the analogy between sin and Aaron and the fallability of their hierarchy; see for example Cornelius a Lapide: Comm. Exod. 32, 5 (ed. cit., p. 578): "Aaronem non defecisse in fidem, sed in professione fidei: sicut Petrus, negans Christum, non perdidit fidem, sed peccavit contra eius confessionem."
[101]See Comm. lat. to Exodus, *ad loc.* (Opera 25, Corp. ref. 53, 81).
[102]Inst. I 11 (ed. cit., vol. 1, p. 130, with variations): "Parquoy l'esprit humain engendre les idoles et la main les enfante. Que telle soit la source d'idolatrie, assaivoir que les hommes ne croyent point que Dieu leus soit prochain, sinon

phrase "Moses saw that the people were naked" (Exod. 32, 35) is taken to mean that they divested themselves of the glory of God.[103]

Of course, the problem of the images' legitimacy marks a point of disagreement between Luther and Calvin. Whereas Luther cannot draw unequivocal conclusions from the episode in Exod. 32,[104] Calvin forthrightly deduces confirmation that the second commandment demands the destruction of every sacred image.[105] But setting aside this difference, the core of Reformist interpretation is identical. Unanimously, the Reformation rereads the story of the idolatry of the people and vigorously reproposes the transcendence of God against all speculation, fantasy and current religious practice.[106]

---

qu'il l'ayent present d'une facon charnelle, il appert par l'example de peuple d'Israel [here he cites Exod. 32]. Ils vouloyent avoir quelque image qui les menast a Dieu, et l'experience monstre tous les jours cela, que la nature de hommes ne se peut tenir quoye [lat. inquietam esse carnem], iusques a ce qu'elle ait rencontre quelque masque ou fantosme respondant a sa follie, pour s'y esiouir [rejoice] comme en la remembrance de Dieu. Et il n'y a eu aage depuis la creation du monde auquel les hommes, pour obeir a ceste cupidite insensee, ne se soit dressez des signes et figures, ausquelles ils ont pense que Dieu se monstrat a aux." See Comm. lat. to Exodus (ed. cit., p. 81).

[103]Serm. sur Michée 70a, ed. Benoit (Neukirchen 1964) p. 75, with adopted parallel texts. Luther was uncertain, but he had also come to a similar decision: see WA 16, 631R.

[104]Deut. Mosi cum annot. (1525) 7, 1-2 (WA 14, 621): "Tertius furor eorum est, quod prorsus omnes imagines perdunt, cum Moses solum de iis praecipiat, quae coluntur et quibus fiditur."

[105]See also Zwingli, for example Von der Kirche (Hauptschriften, vol. 10, Zürich 1963, p.3).

[106]See the discussion immediately after the text cited in note 104, Inst. I 11 (ed. cit., vol. 1, pp. 131 ff). Not even the prior tradition was unanimous on the utilization of Exod. 32 in an aniconic sense. For Germanus of Costantinople it could not be so used: he defends himself against charges of idolatry brought *more iudaico* against the Church (Ep. dogm. 1; PG 98, 153) or even from charges of idolatry from the Jews (Ep. dogm. 4; PG 98, 168). Similarly, Jonah of Orleans defends the cult of the cross against false analogies (De cultu imag. I; PL 106, 337). In Agobard, on the other hand, an aniconic use is found (Lib. imag. sanct. 16; PL 104, 213). He charges contemporary Judaism with idolatry (De iud. superst. 10; PL 104, 86-87). Analagously, the Caroli Magni capitulare de imaginibus notes that "Dominus in montem Sinai descendens legem non pictam, sed scriptam Moysi dedit, et in tabulis lapideis non imagines, sed apices, qui indices rerum sive signa verborum esse perhibentur, tradidit" (II 30; MGH Leg. 2, 2, 93).

Conclusions

The episode of the golden calf underpins the two major questions that the Church faces from the second century onwards, its relationship with rabbinic Judaism and the meaning of the Church's Jewish Scriptures – above all insofar as they are pertinent to the legislative sphere. These two questions, which reveal themselves forcefully even through our briefest contact with ancient Christian theological literature, ensure that attention continues to be paid to the historical-exegetic vicissitudes of the biblical text Exod. 32. The first question bears on the Church's *being*, on its self-awareness and self-image; the second bears on its *having*, on the legacy it can claim for itself. Confronted by an initially hostile world that is ignorant of its existence, in order to give witness of itself, Christianity is forced to recognize that it has in Judaism an elder yet dangerous brother. To avoid all risk of confusion (both from within and without), it must draw up lines of demarcation. Consequently, it can no longer simply appeal to biblical precedents which, by some inscrutable design, overturn the hierarchy, as in Paul: "When they were not yet born and had done neither good nor bad ... it was said to Rebecca: 'The elder will serve the younger,' as it is written: 'I loved Jacob and I hated Esau'" (Rom. 9:11-12). Christianity must now uncover the reasons for this unexpected move, this change of course. And the original apostasy of the people suits this new purpose well. It is used to this end in Barnabas' Epistle, the most ancient anti-Jewish post-biblical text. As we have seen, Barnabas' position is clear cut. To those who dare think that the covenant also belongs to the Jews, he writes: "It is ours, of course; they had already lost it for ever the moment Moses received it" (4:7) – all on account of the golden calf. According to this unknown author, there was no later divine pardon, no renewing of the covenant, no long further history of falls and reconciliations. The history of Israel ends as soon as it begins! Everything that the Jewish Bible later contains pertinent to legal matters is the unique preserve of Christians. And they are called on to read it through a spiritual lens.

As I have suggested, each commentator brings his own perspective to the text, and that perspective is reflected in nuances of interpretation. Not only would it take too long and serve little purpose to underline the many differences, of every kind, that distinguish the positions held by Tertullian, Cyprian, and Origen, beyond the obvious difference of nuances, there is one overriding common element that we must bear in mind. All our commentators determine the theological type of the people as sinful, incredulous, idolatrous – they were already so at the moment of the covenant, according to the pseudo-Barnabas; always so, according to Tertullian; from the very beginning and for ever, according to Origen, who establishes a perfect symmetry between the respective beginnings of the two covenants and the two apostasies. This is the gist of the charge levelled in Stephen's speech that "you always put up resistance to the Holy Spirit: as were your fathers, so are you" (Acts 6:51). But now it stands reified in its historical-theological scheme to such an extent that nothing of the history of Israel may be saved.

Yet things were not so simple. Once the originary deviance of the Jewish people had been established, the two sides could not, despite everything, be so unproblematically kept apart. The second problem, what the church had as its legacy, remained. Christianity depended on Jewish Scripture, which the church could in no way repudiate. From the point of view of the written traditions, the fate of Christianity was inextricably bound up with that of Judaism; on account of its origins, Christianity could not proceed as Islam was to do a few centuries later, and refound traditions and doctrines in a new literary corpus while at the same time denouncing as falsification, or at least as unreliable source, any pre-existing document. Christianity was faced with the opposite problem – how to justify its own Bible, composed as it was of two distinct but not separable documents. At stake was the total incomprehension of the event and of Christian Scripture, which would have been deprived of its historical and doctrinal basis (as happened with gnosticism).

Justification was easy as far as prophetic Scripture was concerned: it was sufficient to follow Jesus' lead, the use he had made of prophetic Scripture, according to the account given in the New Testament; it was possible for sapiential literature, given the tendentially universalistic character of its ethical message. But the operation was far more difficult when the law was at stake, not only because of the demands of the mission, not only because of the original clash between Jesus and

Conclusions

legal traditions (with its tragic consequence), but principally because of a shift in the deepest center of religious experience so that from Paul to John, and perhaps even earlier, to be a believer meant above all sacramental and moral participation in Christ. It did not mean belonging to the people, fidelity to the land, militancy in the law, loyalty to the nation.

Discarding the solution attempted by the gnostics and Marcion, which rejected Old Testament Scripture, the theologians of the second and third centuries moved in two directions, both of which had previously been tried out by non-Christian exegetic practice. On the one hand, the presence of Jewish Scripture, and its hardest pages, could be justified by recourse to a principle of historicization, according to which Scripture was given once again a place of value in the overall balance of a historical economy governed by God. On the other hand, allegory, figurative readings, typology – by which everything could be turned to the advantage of the *hic et nunc* of the Church and the believer – could be used to appropriate the present day meaning. The historicization allowed Christians respectfully to bow down to the past, to the presupposition of a fundamental continuity of generations and traditions, a common human solidarity. Allegory allowed Christians to take over freely what would otherwise have been irreducibly different and unfamiliar and put it to the service of present-day needs.

The episode of originary idolatry plays, then, an important role in the historicist attempts at justifying Christianity's heavy legacy of Jewish law. Justin and Iraenaeus (in the second half of the the second century), the one in close contact with rabbinic Judaism, the other with the gnostic dualism which denied the Old Testament, make use of it to understand the sense of the more specifically Jewish legislation (norms which govern worship and food, for example). Considering the *deuterosis*, the repetition of the law which followed the fall into idolatry (Exod. 32-34), and the differences between this and the former law (Exod. 20), Justin (Dial. 19-20) and Iraenaeus (Adv. Haer. IV 15) both concur that the second law is the result of an "accommodation" to the particular historical contingencies, to the particular degree of development of the people. Divine pedagogy is aware of the necessity to make more precise and concrete demands, to pose more severe limits, even to punish the still too unruly pupil – a point of view shared by Clement of Alexandria at the beginning of the third century. This, I believe, is the beginning of a current of historical thought on Judaism (even though it comes mixed up with a great deal of typology and invective). A current of thought, that is, which while never abolishing its diversity and distance, confidently approaches the past, perceives its analogy and continuity with the present, and recognizes it as its own.

But wherever Christianity's historiographical problem par excellence – the inevitable presence of the document of Jewish Scriptures in the Christian Bible – is addressed through allegorical exegesis, for the believer all distance is abolished, every event is contemporary, all real diversity is jettisoned from either Testament. This, I believe, can be said of Origen and his exegesis, despite his philological sensibility and a certain attention to the historic sense. And, I believe, this can also be said of most ensuing exegesis strongly influenced by Origen. Here, not one fragment of ancient Scripture is lost, each letter takes on its full sense, it reveals its "truth." But with the purging from the text of the historical distance, facilitated by allegory, the distance becomes absolute and takes on the guise of irreducible otherness. The letter cannot be used unless it gives meaning. And the overall Jewish experience, made of flesh, seed, blood, wandering and error, law, transgression, reconciliation, will only produce meaning when "sterilized," when radically transposed into Christian spirituality. It is not surprising, therefore, that an in-depth historical analysis into Origen's reading of the first idolatrous fall and on the historical turning point of the deuterosis is not attempted. What is said – and this is the most important pronouncement on the subject, one to be taken over by later Christian exegesis – is only that the broken tablets are the figure of the end of the first covenant. This abridgement reveals the basic lack of interest for all too human events. Origenian exegesis does, nonetheless, have the upper hand. So the overall effect is a reification of the split, as Christianity sees it, between Jewish Scripture and the people that bears it; Scripture is completely assimilated, taken over by spiritual people who understand its spiritual sense; the Jewish People belongs by now to some useless prehistory. The result does not substantially differ from that already sketched out by Barnabas' Epistle.

Between the fourth and fifth centuries the separation of Bible and people, of Christianity and Judaism is further consolidated by the social and political transformations which give Christianity a dominating social role.

Christianity, whose superior spirituality is now incarnated in an entire concrete, social group – the monastic ranks – rudely points its finger at the carnality of Judaism in terms that are no longer theological but also now psychological and cultural. The golden calf episode plays a crucial role in this context, too, as an index to the changes and degeneration in a relationship. Some commentators (Athanasius, Cyril of Alexandria and, later between the seventh and eighth centuries, John of Damascus), following the model of sapiential polemic and, in part, Stephen's speech, attribute the idolatrous fall to an intellectual travesty. The words that Paul, quoting Wisdom, reserves for the pagans in the first chapter of the letter to the Romans are applied to the Jews. But it is above all the base, carnal, sensual root of sin that is highlighted. And here Paul's *epithymia-concupiscentia* (1 Cor. 10) is fully in force. Consider the Christian spirituality of Ambrose, Jerome, Augustine (who here takes his place in a moralistic, African tradition), Basil and John Chrysostom. It takes the form of a sharp contrast between the sublime ascetic-mystic spirituality of Moses and the baseness of the carnal people, the unleashing of their instinctive eating, drinking, *lusus*. Chrysostom's invective has an especially rough edge insofar as it sketches out and foregrounds the Jewish psychological type – to which he even adds the same bestial connotations associated with the animal they falsely worshipped. Although Chrysostom's invective is a rhetorical operation dictated by pressing pastoral concerns, it is no less excusable given the burden of threat and violence which was to be its legacy to history.

So in these years, the idea is consolidated that the Egyptian Apis was worshipped in the form of a calf's head at the foot of Mt. Sinai. This manoeuvre constitutes one more way to inveigh against the Jews and then turn on them the charge of zoolatry which, in the past, the pagans had applied against both Jews and Christians.

Although a straight line is drawn that retrospectively connects the sin at the foot of Mt. Sinai with the sin of Adam, and prospectively links it to Calvary, the accompanying Christian polemic grows more truculent and destructive. Paradoxically, the increasingly negative tone demands that someone be saved. That someone is Aaron, who is now guarded by the same apologetic protective net as had been afforded to him by preceding and contemporary Jewish tradition. To this end, the commentators adopt certain expedients. From Ephraem on, they refer to the death of Hur.

In the fourth and fifth centuries, the stereotype of Jewish carnality, reinforcing and reflecting the current juridically sanctioned situation of dependency and inferiority, is definitively put in place. The logic is as follows: sacred history, beginning with the repression which followed the fall into idolatry, confirmed the image of the servile people. Yet it confirmed servitude, not suppression. Evidently, then (to Jerome, and Augustine), Christianity must watch over the survival of Judaism. But it must watch over it not just because the Jews offer a sort of living proof of the authenticity of Jewish writings, not just because their dispersion and servile condition offer proof of the fulfillment of the prophecies against Israel, not just because, as Paul argues, their future conversion must be foreseen, but in more general terms because – on the basis of the above – the presence of the Jewish community, no matter how degraded and miserable, is useful to the internal economy of Christian ideology (even more than to the external economy, the means of production).

In sum: the Jewish people are the enabling condition for an operation which leads to the definition by antithesis of a Christian self-image. Christianity rests its case on this self-image achieved by contrast, thereby reserving for itself the sublime spaces of spirituality, and leaving to Judaism the base and vulgar space of carnality. If the separation of the spheres, in the first theological controversy, was purely theoretical, and Christians and Jews found themselves side by side in a minority situation in and around their contemporary society, with the ideological and political domination of Christianity, the separation takes on the new and more concrete forms of an ethical, psychological and (in the broadest terms) cultural order, strengthened by political practice and legislative support, taking on the fixed totalizing characteristics of ideology, from which one can extract new guidelines as times and situations change.

The history of the idolatrous episode's interpretation and the uses to which the episode is put, so important in the first anti-Jewish controversies, have, it seems to me, allowed us to trace the formation, consolidation and determination of the stereotypical opposition between carnality and spirituality as fundamental modalities of ecclesial self-awareness in the late ancient world. The hermeneutic efficacy of this key theme diminishes in the next centuries; it does not seem to me to progress beyond repetitions with variations. (I am not so enamored of this literature as to want to guide my readers around the numerous sites where the theme resurfaces in the anti-Jewish controversy – even if in the preceding chapter I have often extended the analysis well beyond the fifth century in order to mark the almost unchanged persistence of exegetic schemes.) Even the use of *ratio* in the arguments beginning in the twelfth century, or, a little later, the more direct knowledge of the adverse sources, in Raymond Martini, Nicholas of Lyra and Dionysius the Carthusian, do not substantially modify the picture. The division of the available space is now fully achieved; the two great regions – spirit and flesh – have now been demarcated and nothing, I would dare say, can threaten the security of the obsessively reiterated border-lines.

But there is, in truth, a new approach. And here, once again, the golden calf acts as a useful index. The Moses/people opposition is used *intra ecclesia* to found and endorse a separation that this time permeates the whole hierarchical system and stands between ascetes and people. Again, the roots are remote (formerly in Tertullian and Origen, later, in the forth century, in Basil, Chrysostom, Jerome, Augustine – behind whom one can recognize Philo). This approach views Moses on high; the people down below on the plain. On high it reads compunction, prayer, fasting, contemplation, ecstasy; down below it sees destructive exaltation, confusion, corruption of the belly, excessive *lusus*, anarchy. The biblical scene suggests and reinforces the classic contrast between ascetes, monastic saints and pastors of the soul (who conform to Moses' model), and vulgar, incontinent masses deprived of any leader or law.

In the originary lesson of Exodus, Moses harshly punishes the sin. He then reconstitutes the egalitarian unity of the people on the basis of a more adequate law which channels their needs but does not suppress them. In the ecclesial and monastic lesson, we find two levels. On one level, there are those who, at the cost of repressing *voluptas*, enjoy the privilege of commerce with God and a certain participation in the powers of Moses; on another, like the Israelites on the plain, are those to whom is conceded or even delegated a certain guilty commerce with the flesh, the things of the world – at the cost of a little sweat on the brow. This is an inevitable concession necessary for the survival of Christianity. Here, then, once again, is a theological reading which takes as its ideological basis a separation, in which the Pauline metaphor of the body of Christ, which supposes an organic symbiosis, a vital reciprocal exchange, is shaped to cover over the reality of a parasitical dependence of the high on the low. When Moses comes down order is ensured and justice imposed on the heretics, by way of the Levites; the sublime spirituality of the one does not go without the "slavery without name" of the others, who are infinitely more numerous.

The effect, then, of the claimed separation between flesh and spirit is twofold. On the one hand, under this cover and with great protestations of total non-culpability, the church can often carry out the most grandiose of theological/political operations without even being aware, one might say, of being confused with the ancient Israel. On the other, it can repudiate any comparison with the considerations and reasons of those vital forms of Judaism which had survived. The Church can relegate Judaism to a servile condition, giving it those functions that are least worthy because incompatible with Christian nobility and spirituality; it can even confer on Judaism subhuman "bestial" attributes (I refer to John Chrysostom's texts and to their wide circulation in the slavonic translation, where their historical function and their destructive capacity can be understood). All this can happen – with the exception of historical revenge and the inventive possibilities that the segregation and forced contact with materiality that Christianity had abandoned could concede to Jewish intelligence.

All this is ancient and medieval history. But we have seen how the secularized West, up to and including Hegel, Feuerbach and Marx, has in fact welcomed and made abundant use of the stereotypes elaborated by the anti-Jewish polemic. A word should be said of Marx. His *On the Jewish Question* (1843) shares with Feuerbach, and makes even more coarse and insulting, the Hegelian definition of Judaism as a religion of "Practical need, selfishness."[1] It is Marx himself who perfectly delineates, from his standpoint (where the historical and religious terms have other meanings as metaphors for bourgeois society), the above-mentioned process:

> Christianity has overcome real Judaism in appearance only. It was too gentlemanly, too spiritual, to remove the crudeness of practical need other than by raising it into the blue heavens.
>
> Christianity is the sublime thought of Judaism; Judaism is the vulgar practical application of Christianity. But this practical application could only become universal after Christianity as the perfect religion had completed, in a theoretical manner, the self-alienation of man from himself and from nature.[2]

Here, there is everything. We encounter the separation of the spheres – "theoretical" and "practical," carnal and spiritual; the spiritualistic self-alienation of Christianity; the revenge of those material instances that had been scornfully removed, or delegated to others.

I would, however, like to return to the origins of the phenomenon that I have been describing. In launching its critique of Jewish carnality, the Christian polemic had access to a potent weapon, the protest of the prophets against the dullness and blindness of Israel, its baseness, its surrender to idolatry, its ritualism, its coarseness, its complete incomprehension of the intellectual and ethical instances of Mosaic monotheism. Indeed, the use of Old Testament prophets, and the prophetic use (as a function of Christ and the Church) of all Scripture, including the historical books, had characterized Jesus' preaching (much more than Paul's and the first generation of Christians). Consequently, it can neither surprise nor cause scandal that right from the beginning Christians read all the Jewish Bible and applied it to themselves ("it has been written for us") and received the events of the past as "shadow" and "figure" of the present, no matter how irritating this may have been for those who felt their Scripture

---

[1] Marx (1843) p. 58 (MEW 1, 374).
[2] Ibid., p. 61 (MEW 1, 374).

Conclusions

had been misappropriated. It is a normal hermeneutic operation contingent on a moment of religious renewal: an operation which ancient and more recent Jewish history often exemplifies abundantly when it testifies to the vitality of the monotheistic Mosaic tradition. The operation ceases to be legitimate when it repudiates the direct relationship with contemporary Judaism and when the anti-Jewish polemic exploits the ancient Scriptures in order to judge and condemn Judaism, as happens in Chrysostom.[3]

An even more serious consequence derives from a certain literal reading where the "growth of Scripture with he who reads," of which Gregory the Great speaks[4] (in other words, a creative hermeneutics), is no longer at stake. In its place stands the loss of contact, under the profile of religious anthropology, with the meaning of the doctrinal contents and the Jewish religious experience. This basic datum must here be remembered: primitive Christianity takes over Jewish Scripture to the letter; unlike Islam, it does not work an integral "rewriting" of Jewish (and Christian) traditions for the benefit of the new religion, nor does it attempt to justify such a move by citing Jewish (and Christian) falsifications of the originary Scriptures, to which access can no longer be had (this charge of falsification also appears in the Jewish-Christian controversy, but has a far more minor role); instead, it takes over an imposing and many-sided literary corpus *en masse*. This is the case not only because of the use Jesus makes of it; not only because of the messianic testimonies it holds; not only because of the Jewish roots of the first Christian movement, but because without Jewish Scripture Christianity loses its fundamental doctrinal basis on man, on the world, on the single God, on the beginning, on the end. To lose contact with these premises means to lose Christianity altogether, reduce it to an intellectualism divorced from any consideration of the material basis of existence – gnosis. And not by chance the anti-gnostic struggle, above all with Iraenaeus, produces thoughts which I consider among the most important in Christian theology. I have given an example in the course of the present work. From that example one can perhaps glimpse the overall movement of this current of thought – man in his entirety, body, soul and spirit which God forms and educates progressively, respecting his times and concrete needs.

By accusing Origen of spiritualism, of the operation as a result of which the entire Old Testament is at once re-endowed with its

---

[3]The best work is by Simon (1948) pp. 166 ff (on John Chrysostom, pp. 256 ff).
[4]See now Bori (1987).

spiritual and mystic sense[5] and emptied and purged of its earth, flesh and blood; by turning against Augustine the same basic charge, aggravated by the most explicit translation in an ecclesiological and institutional sense of the mystic Origenian apparatus; by reproaching the monasticism of East and West with having spread and reinforced this mystic and spiritualistic resolution of the Old Testament and having imposed its hegemony for centuries – saying all this, I realize that I have simplified many things which, from a historical point of view, are more complex (a single example: is there not Philo behind Origen?) I realize that I am flying in the face of many objections and, much worse, contravening the *pietas* towards those masters of patristic ressourcement whose insignia is the reevaluation of Origenian and medieval exegesis (I am thinking above all of De Lubac).

It has not been my purpose to construct an apology for Judaism. The same operations that I wanted to highlight apropos of historical Christianity can easily be seen in historical Judaism;[6] it would be sufficient, in fact, to have tagged onto the prophetic criticism and onto the "hypocrisy" that Jesus attacked. Here, however, I have been interested in observing the phenomenon of the hypocrisy that invades that movement which was born precisely to denounce hypocrisy.

Neither do I intend, by highlighting and criticizing the spiritualistic evolutions, to return to Christianity some authentic essence, one that is close to Judaism. As I have been saying, originary Christianity already bears the sign of a change that is clearly in the exclusive reference to Jesus, a historic person, transfigured by faith – a reference that finds neither comparison nor correspondence in Jewish religious structures, nor in Moses. It is from this situation that spring two different cultural anthropologies – for example, their respective answers to sin. To the sin of the lust (*epithymia*) of the people, the answer for Moses lies in intervention, in punishment, in repentance, in the renewal of the pact (Exod. 32-34); against lust, Paul (Rom. 7-8) proposes entry into the sphere of dominion, of belonging to the resuscitated Christ. In the first case, discipline is proposed; in the second, the image of Christ dominates. In the first, the space proposed is that of the people and the earth; in the second, it comprises the body

---

[5]In Num. hom. 9,4 (GCS 30, 59): "The one and the other for us is the New Testament, not for its temporal age but for the innovation of its intelligence."

[6]A single example taken from the anti-Christian polemic: the Christians say that the Jews erred when they worshipped a clean thing such as a golden object, but they err even more when they hold that something holy can enter into something dirty like the belly of a woman. See Nizzahon vetus, Pentat. 39 (ed. D. Berger, *The Jewish-Christian Debate in the High Middle Ages*, Philadelphia 1979, pp. 67 ff).

Conclusions

of Christ. In the first, the Spirit opens the way to the achievement of the law; in the second, it makes it possible to know and belong to Christ.

Let me add this last warning: the critique of spiritualism is not, on its own, a critique of religion, far less a critque of mysticism. Without the mystic experience of Moses, Jesus, Paul and, in a certain sense, Mohammed, there would be no "biblical" monotheisms. At the same time we must be aware of the specific terms of these mystical experiences. They always maintain, at their origins, a distance between divinity and creature (God is "in the heavens," man on the earth). They do not offer themselves as research into the divine as such – remember Calvin's critique of idolatry, of "men who do not believe that God is their neighbor unless he is present to them in flesh." Rather, in their originary manifestation – and therefore their exemplary and reiterable manifestations – they situate themselves beyond the given order, proposing different and ever more humanly adequate answers to the needs of a people, drawing on God's transcendence over the existing order and thus admitting the transgression of this order.

The main phenomenon with which this work has been concerned is not, however, the historic or mystic distance between the two religions, Jewish and Christian. Rather, my concern has been with the more precise phenomenon of the early construction of the abstract image of Judaism as an exponent of carnality, an image which met the needs of Christianity and furnished a guarantee and reassurance of Christianity's superior spiritual extraction to such a point that any affinity or common ground between the two peoples is denied. We see no relation between father and son, still less between brothers, rather a polar opposition, like that of flesh and spirit, begotten and unbegotten. Luther, at the point and moment of the fracture (*confractio*), opposes all his weight and all the materiality of his language (alongside which only Rabelais can stand comparison) to these things. Although we can also charge him with incoherence (his mode of dealing with the Jews is a prime example), his insight remains crucial. He writes: "their most spiritual moments, as they dream, are not only of the flesh, but also mightily impious."[7] Impiety is not in the "flesh," still less in the "spirit" but in the travesty of carnal thoughts in the garb of spiritual thoughts.

---

[7] WA 40/2, 111 Dr: "Ideo eorum cogitationes spiritualissimae – ut somniant – non solum sunt carnalissimae, sed etiam impiissimae, quia, excluso et contempto verbo, fide, Christo etc., fiducia propriae iustitiae volunt peccata eludere, gratiam et vitam aeternam consequi."

Appendix I

The Golden Calf in the Biblical Tradition and in the Koran

1. The Old Testament

From even the simplest attempt to sum up the facts, it emerges that the biblical account, as presented in chapters 32-34 of Exodus, is full of dark corners, contradictions and problems. Chapter 33 contains elements that do not square with the rest (33:1-6: God will not come with the people; the people must divest themselves of their ornaments). Furthermore, God first seems to refuse to walk in the midst of the people (33:3) but then agrees to do so (33:14-17). (Even earlier [32:34], however, He had said: "My angel will go before you," not God Himself.) More than that: we read, "Jahweh spoke face to face with Moses, as one man speaks to another" (33:11); but, a little later, God tells Moses that he will not be able to see his face, because no-one can look on it and stay alive (33:20). There are other examples: God orders Moses to write the second tablets, while previously He had said: "I shall write" (34:1.28). And why does God say "I shall write on these tablets the words that were on the first tablets," when the prescriptions are different (34: 10-28)? In what do the "words of the covenant, the ten words" (34:28) consist? And what is the shining of the skin of Moses' face (heb. *qaran*, Vulg. *cornutus*, Septuagint *dedoxasmene*). What is this phenomenon that requires that he be veiled before the people may approach him?

And if we limit our range to chapter 32, we may ask, for example, the following list of questions: How is the calf made from the precious material offered by the people? What does Aaron mean when, after throwing the gold into the fire, he says the simulacrum "came out of it"? What is this "form" – thus translated, according to custom, from the Hebrew *hrt* – with which Aaron models the statue? Who is the image supposed to replace – God or Moses? Why is it said "Make us elohim, because we do not know what has happened to that man Moses, *who brought us out* from the land of Egypt," yet also: "Here are your elohim, Israel, that *brought you out* from the land of Egypt" (32:1.4)? How does Aaron's betrayal square with the role he is given elsewhere in Exodus as collaborator and "prophet" of Moses (7:1), coparticipant in the experiences and revelations which are addressed to him, and permanent head of the priesthood (29:9)? In what does the play, the revelry of the people consist? What about its "mockery?" Whence come the sons of Levi, absent from the betrayal yet authors of the cold-blooded repression? Where were they before? And what is the reference when God speaks of the "day of his visit" when He will punish the people for their sin (32:34)?

Contemporary exegesis tackles this forest of enigmas with the weapons supplied by literary criticism, history of tradition and redaction, on the one hand, and with historical-religious comparative studies, on the other. Even though this kind of inquiry does not fall within the boundaries of the present work, which hinges more properly and primarily on the Christian interpretive tradition, it would be remiss of me not to summarize the most important data pertinent to recent discussion. The so-called documentary theory attempts to resolve the contradictions by showing how they come from different documents and traditions (the Yahwist and the Elohist). According to this view, the repetition of the covenant following the apostasy is the result of an artificial systematization that has sought to preserve both the first account of the covenant (Exod. 24: Elohist) and the second (Exod. 34, Yahwist). In particular, the documentary approach argues that the presence of contradictory elements in Exod. 32 may be explained by the incomplete fusion of different sources. Thus it accounts for the two different ways Moses learns of the apostasy (vv. 11-14, 30-34); the different consequences contingent on the apostasy (vv. 14-15, 20, 28, 34-35); the fact that the calf's manufacture is attributed on various occasions to Aaron who grants the people's demand (v. 4), to the people (vv. 8 and 20), to both the people and Aaron (v. 35), and to either Aaron or the fire (v. 24: "I threw it into the fire and out came the calf").

But concerning both the accurate identification of the different documentary elements that make up the text, and their historical background, there is still a great deal of uncertainty.[1] So much so, that an opposite tendency, one not founded on literary criticism, seems to underline that the contradictions are only apparent. From this perspective, "the story of the making and the destruction of the calf may, in a literary sense, be considered a unified account if we forget the difficulties that come from our modern constructions and pay attention to the models of thought which were dominant in ancient Canaan." Following these models, we register no contradiction in the fact that the making of the sacred object is attributed at the same time to different subjects (Aaron, the people, the fire), or that the destruction takes place in ways that seem incompatible.[2] And the historical-religious perspective points out that a lunar cult, perhaps transferred from Harran by some of Israel's antecedents, was alive at least until the Mosaic period.[3] It has also been argued strongly that the golden calf is a variant on the "cherubims," the pedestals on which the invisible Jahweh rests[4] (whereas the theory of an Egyptian origin to the simulacrum has tended to die away).[5]

The history of traditions and historical context, under whose aegis the redaction of the text as we read it today falls, underlines the inevitable correlation of the story of the golden calf in Exod. 32 to the account of the two golden calves erected by Jeroboam at Betel and at Dan (1 Kings 12). Smolar and Aberbach write:

---

[1]For literary analysis, following the documentary hypothesis, see above all Noth (1958) pp. 200-02: the prevalence of a Yahwist source, with various additions, Exod. 32:9-14 deuteronomist and 32:21-29; Lewy (1959): Yahwist source, with various deuteronomist and sacerdotal additions; Lehming (1960): complex proposal, summed up in the table on p. 50 of his work; Beyerlin (1961): prevalence of the Elohist source; Jaros (1974, pp. 372-88) follows Beyerlin; Childs (1974) insists on the literary unity, with a probably Yahwist primary source and two expansions, 32:7-14 deuteronomist, 32:25-29 independent source; difficulties of specific attributions: Hahn (1981) p. 140 and table at pp. 142 ff.

[2]Loewenstamm (1967) pp. 489 ff and 483 ff following the Ugaritic account of the destruction of Mot by 'Anat. For this account see also Fensham (1966) and Hvidberg-Hansen (1971). Loewenstamm's position has been challenged by Perdue (1973), to which Loewenstamm (1975) has replied by reasserting the literary coherence of Exod. 32:4, 20, 24 (but which, for the author, does not mean to deny the "complicated prehistory of the whole of chapter 32," p. 330).

[3]See Bailey (1971) pp. 107-15, particularly p. 114; see also Sasson (1968) who connects the golden calf with the cult of the bull and the calf who, as symbols of fertility and strength, were present in Accadic and Amorreic milieux associated with Sin and by the Caanans with Baal. The author also explains in this way Moses' facies cornuta. See now Hahn (1981) pp. 336 ff.

[4]Hahn (1981) pp. 332-34.

[5]See Bailey (1971) p. 97 note 3 (with ample doxography) and p. 102 note 30; Jaros (1974) p. 381; Hahn (1981) pp. 314 ff.

There are so many similarities between the two accounts that the dependence of the one upon the other can hardly be doubted. In the formation of the calf cult, the building of the altar, the offering of the sacrifices, the role of the Levites, the description of the new cult as the sin par excellence, and the resultant divine displeasure, which leads to the national disaster, the two accounts are remarkably similar in tendency, language, and style. Hence, conservative scholars assume that Jeroboam revived an ancient cult harking back to Aaron, whom he took as his model in all his cultic activities, even going so far as to name his two sons, Nadab and Abijah (=Abiahu=Abihu), after Aaron's eldest sons.[6]

A more radical and controversial position, one which has been contested, argues that the story of the golden calf (Exod. 32) draws essentially on 1 Kings 12, and reflects the polemic with the local baalim. The polemical intention of Exod. 32 against Jeroboam and the separatist cult of the calves at Betel and Dan is not contested; Jeroboam did not introduce a new cult of Canaan origins, but probably recuperated an ancient cult that found its legitimization in its references to Aaron.[7] The latter position, then, argues that the polemic evidences a period during which the priesthood did not yet lay claim to an Aaronide descent.[8] But it is denied that Jeroboam's calves are the basis of the *ex novo* creation of Exod. 32, in the mode of an aetiological projection. For Exod. 32, this is probably an ancient tradition, independent of the traditions that revolve around the "murmuring" in the desert (and whose victim is Aaron).[9] It is a pre-deuteronomic tradition, pulled into the orbit of the primary source (whether that source is Yahwist or Elohist is still a bone of contention), and incorporated successively into the section of Exod. 32-34 by the redactor.[10] This, then, is a tradition from a more ancient apostasy, the archetype of all successive acts of infidelity, and could not have arisen from 1 Kings 12 alone.[11]

Finally, let me rehearse some exegetic details concerning Exod. 32:1-6. In v. 1 we read of "that Moses, the man who brought us out." The appellation "man" (*ha-ish*) is also found elsewhere, with authoritative tones (Exod. 11:3; Num. 12:3: "the man Moses"). Here, the tone is strengthened by the demonstrative *zeh*, "that Moses." In v. 4 the

---

[6] See Smolar and Aberbach (1976) who synthesize the earlier Aberbach and Smolar (1967).
[7] See Jaros (1974) pp. 381 ff.
[8] See Smolar and Aberbach (1976) p. 123, who synthesize the earlier Aberbach and Smoler (1967) pp. 134-40.
[9] See Coats (1968) p. 191.
[10] Childs (1974) pp. 560 ff.
[11] Beyerlin (1961) p. 145; Schmid (1968) p. 81.

Appendix I

calf (*egel*) appears. Some commentators see a nuance in the use of this term (instead of "bull"), but the question remains open. More controversial is the sense of what, for example, has often been rendered as: "he took them from their hands and *moulded them into a form*, and made from it a moulded calf" (the translated version of which I have provisionally followed here). Of particular difficulty is *wayyasar oto ba heret*. To what does *oto* refer – the gold or the calf? What does *heret* mean? (From a comparison with Is 8:1 it would mean "instrument for engraving," "stylus," and not "form.") What does *wayyasar* mean? (It may be *qal* of *swr* or *hiphil* of *srr*, both in the sense of "tighten," "constrain," while the usual verb to mean "form" is *ysr*.) Noth's proposed solution is to read *harit* as "bag," following 2 Kings 5:23, with a slight textual change. We should now take the passage to mean "and he collected the gold in a cloak or bag."[12] But as this interpretation involves an intervention in the text this solution has been contested by other commentators. Certainly, from the standpoint of the narrative, it does appear to be inadequate. I prefer: "he gave it form with a chisel." We would have, then, a *hysteron proteron*, the finishing touches before the moulding.[13] "Here are your elohim" can be taken as singular or plural (your god or your gods); the problem is, in fact, connected to the relationship one wants to establish with 1 Kings 12:28, Jeroboam's *two* golden calves. And what of v. 6, "revelry" (*lesaheq*)? It can have the meaning both of play as sport (Judg. 16:25) and play as sexual activity (Gen. 26:8; 39:14). This latter meaning is preferred by recent commentators and by the targums.

What emerges at the end of this intricate itinerary? Most of the questions that were initially raised are probably destined to remain unanswered in any unequivocal way. Since I can offer only a personal, albeit hypothetical, point of view on the question, let me answer in such terms. An ancient tradition, independent from those traditions relative to the murmuring of the people in the desert, transmits the memory of the people's surrender and places it chronologically at the same time as the gift of the covenant. The surrender, then, not only occupies a place in the order of the events of the stipulation, but also upsets and problematizes them. This tradition passes a judgment of condemnation of Aaron's role and sees in the symbolism of the calf an

---

[12] See Noth (1959); Petuchowski (1960): Rashi also knows this possible interpretation; Loewenstamm (1967) p. 485, with further supporting elements in the Targum pseudo-Jonathan (of which more later); see Cassuto (1951) and Noth (1959) *ad loc*.

[13] See Childs (1974) pp. 555 ff: "and shaped it with an engraving tool." This is the solution of the Seventy and of Onqelos. See Hahn (1981) pp. 145 ff.

idolatrous betrayal. It is unlikely that this event, massively counterproductive for the entire people, and for Aaron in particular, was created *ad hoc* to condemn Jeroboam's actions. But it is just as difficult to imagine that this same tradition, with all its strongly negative connotations, could be used positively by Jeroboam to justify his religious politics and the erection of the two golden calves at Betel and Dan. Given the ambivalent nature of the original facts, there must have been another more practicable version. The facts, as well as giving a radically negative evaluation (idolatry), could also give the following positive justification: in other words, the utilization, which goes back to Aaron, of a taurine symbolism connected to God and belonging to the fathers and to Moses (not then Apis, but not even originally the Canaan *baalim*). Jeroboam refers to this positive version of the facts at the institution of the rival cult. But the orthodox cult which emerges victorious (whether Elohist or Yahwist is difficult to tell) opposes this version. This tradition is taken up later by Deuteronomist preaching (Deut. 9), of which traces in Exod. 32:11-13 are recognizable.

A historical-critical discussion would serve very little purpose if it aimed only to attenuate the perception of the unique gravity of the facts that the Bible unhesitatingly narrates – the tragedy of a "no" that follows on the heels of the "yes" of the covenant, the destruction of the covenant, and the elimination of the figure of its mediator, Moses. In truth, it is the people who break the tablets! But more than that, the confused order of the narrated events in chapters 33 and 34, and the many enigmas they contain, must not prevent us from grasping the essence of the history, the overturning of the catastrophe with the renewal of the covenant and the return of Moses to his glorious role.

This nucleus and substance remain in the collective memory and embark on a long journey, that I would here like to trace. First, this memory persists in Jewish biblical literature: in Moses' long, prophetic and predicatory monologue in Deuteronomy – in the "national lament" of Psalms; in the penitential prayer, to which Nehemiah refers, on the return from exile and the renewing of the pact.

In the passage from Deuteronomy (9:7-29), Moses is even more alone, even closer to God (forty days and forty nights are spent with him). Man of prayer, great mediator, he is contrasted all the more sharply with the people and their "great sin" (a term which is here used much more insistently than in Exodus). First, he breaks the tablets, then turns to God, destroys the idol (burnt, crumbled, cast on the water, but not swallowed as in Exodus). To the ecstatic transparency of the great mediator is contrasted the dullness of the people, its obstinacy, its "stubbornness." A mode of expression, this, that probably has its origin

Appendix I 91

in Deuteronomy, and from there takes its place in the version found in Exod. 32:9-13. This formula is repeated on countless occasions both in prophetic self-criticism and in the Christian polemic against Judaism.

> They made for themselves a calf on Horeb, they laid down before an image of moulded metal, they exchanged their glory for the figure of an ox which eats grass. They forgot God who had saved them, who had worked great things in Egypt, prodigious things in the country of Ham, terrible things near the Red Sea. And he had already decided to exterminate them, unless Moses his elected one had not stood in the breach, to divert his anger away from the extermination.

Thus Psalm 105 (vv. 19-23), a "historical" psalm, is full of grave reminders ("we have sinned against our fathers, we were impious and perverse" [v. 6]), despite the received benefits. The reasons for this recognition are dwelt on but only to denounce the ingratitude: with words similar to those found in Deuteronomy, the event in Exod. 32 is recalled. Aaron and his responsibilities, however, do not make an appearance (nor will they elsewhere in either the Christian or Jewish Bibles). (A little earlier (v. 16), he had been present beside Moses as the "one consecrated by the Lord.") There is one characteristic of the theological interpretation of the idolatrous phenomenon that recalls the polemic against idolatry carried out by the sapiential books. It appears in the following: "They exchanged their glory [originally this was probably "his" glory, the glory of God] for the figure of a bull which eats hay." Here the denunciation involves ignorance, blindness, foolishness, *agnosia*, as a much later classic text – Wisd. 13 – says. But not, as in the prophetic texts, disobedience, stubbornness, thick-headedness. These are two aspects of the anti-idolatrous polemic which are not separable from a theoretical standpoint and which, although often entwined in texts (as here), are also distinct as concerns origin, literary tone, destination. What remains of the reading of the psalm is the "classical" contrast between divine goodness and forgetfulness, oblivion, ingratitude of the people. Moses stands alone, on the "front line."

Lastly, Nehemiah. Here, exiles who have regained their homeland celebrate the day of expiation. In this penitential clime, a great prayer recalls the infidelity of the people, and divine mercy. The sins of the people are summed up, on the one hand, in the idolatrous episode, on the other by the killing of the prophets. But to both the one sin and the other follows pardon:

> Even when they made for themselves a calf of moulded metal and said: "Here is your God that brought you from Egypt!" and they insulted You gravely, You in your mercy did not abandon them in the desert: the column of cloud that covered them never ceased to guide

them through the day on their path and the column of fire did not cease to light up the way on which they travelled by night (Neh. 9:18-19).

If the illustration of the benefits, against which is contrasted arrogance, stubbornness, ingratitude, forgetfulness, recalls Christian "abuse," the constancy of mercy is punctually restated, so that the same benefits (column of cloud, column of fire, divine teaching, manna, water) are preserved.

2. The New Testament

The point of view reflected in Christian Scripture is different on this score. The two circumstances in which the memory of the idolatrous episode emerges – the first letter to the Corinthians and Acts,[14] of which more later – are extremely different, but the common element is that of a pitiless reminder. But Christian Scripture omits not only the generic attenuating circumstances but also what follows, the divine pardon according to which the history of the people, despite everything, continues.

Paul writes to the Corinthians; he reproaches them, reminds them of what happened to the fathers (1 Cor. 10:6-13). He does not want here to polemicize with the Jews; rather, his goal is to make the members of the community feel insecure. Remember, he suggests, sacramental practice is no guarantee against falls (he spoke of this in chapter 8 and speaks again of it immediately afterwards, in the context of the meats offered to the idols, which must not be eaten in too complacent a manner). The warning that previously (at the end of chapter 9) had been buttressed by an agonistic metaphor (even Paul himself is careful, vigilant, always "in training" in order not to be "disqualified") rests now on memory and is broadened to include the example of "our fathers." The privileges and divine protection during the exodus were enjoyed by all (the cloud, the miraculous crossing of the Red Sea, the manna, the water). Still, "God was not pleased by most of them and so they were struck down in the desert" (10:5). This is an example (*typos*, in the plural; "prefigurations," one could say) for the Corinthian community so that its believers do not "desire bad things as they

---

[14]On the use of the Old Testament in Acts, the bibliography is enormous: see Bovon (1978) pp. 89-117; Schneider (1980) vol. 1, pp. 441 ff; on Stephen, see Bovon (1978) pp. 365-69; among the many contributions, Simon (1958) pp. 38-58 is relevant for the purposes of the present work. For 1 Cor. 10, as well as the commentaries, see Marthelet (1956) pp. 519 ff. Both for Acts 7 and for 1 Cor. 10, it does not seem to me that there have been contributions which are relevant to the use of Exod. 32.

Appendix I

desired them" (in Num. 11:4.34 and at Ps. 105:4 the Greek version speaks of the people's sin of desire in the desert, *epithymian epithymein*). This desire, this *concupiscentia* (as the latin tradition renders *epithymia*) seems, according to Paul, to form a general category of transgression, which gathers up all the sins successively enumerated, of which the first is idolatry – "Do not become idolatrous like some of them, according to what is written: 'the people sat down to eat and drink and rose to make revelry'" [Exod. 32:6]. Other sins, fornication, provocation, murmuring are also recalled.

What is important to understand here is the psychological-moralistic resolution of idolatry as surrender to passions. Eating and drinking prefigure idolatrous revelry (*paizein*: the interpretation of this latter term in the sense of idolatry was current at the time). This notion of idolatry, connected to sexual intemperance and in general terms to the surrender to instincts, also emerges elsewhere in Paul (see Gal. 5:20 and Phil. 3:19; for avarice or *pleonexia*, see Eph. 5:5; Col. 3:5). But note: as the text is not turned against the Jews, it cannot be said that Paul makes the charge of idolatry, and idolatry in this sense, a central element in his discussion with Judaism. When he does speak with Judaism, as in Rom. 2, he uses classic deuteronomic and prophetic terminology, writing "with your hardness and the impenitence of your heart you accumulate anger for the day of anger" (v. 5). In this context of prophetic invective, the accusation of idolatry appears alongside adultery, but without that psychological-moralistic resolution of which I spoke of earlier. When Paul deals at length with the problem of Israel in Romans 9-11, it is equally not a question of *epithymia-concupiscentia*, of corrupt instinctiveness, but of a free, paradoxical choice by God. God, in a certain sense, has changed his plans, despite the gifts and the promises made to "Israel according to the flesh." To this choice, to this election one can either bow down one's head, with the obedience of faith, or remain incredulous, obstinate (Rom. 11:7.25: *porosis*). But divorced from its context which, as I have said, is not anti-Jewish, the passage from 1 Cor. 10 lent itself to the sometimes less than noble purposes of ensuing Christian exegesis. On the one hand, it served for many years as a justification of a banal and generic definition of idolatry as submission to passions of every kind. On the other hand, it is used to confirm (and often determine) the degradation of the nation of "Israel according to the flesh" to a stock marked by sensuality and blind surrender to instincts. In this way, up until Luther, the "works of the flesh" will be taken in a crudely moralistic sense.

In contrast, Stephen, the first martyr, according to the account of Acts, addresses the Jews with a long, lucid and hard-hitting discourse which, for severity, contrasts sharply with his mildness on the point of death. He brings three charges against the Jews. First, is the "making (*moschopoiein*) of the calf"; the second concerns the Temple; the third, the killing of prophets and Jesus. The first charge is formulated thus:

> Moses is he who, while they were gathered in the desert, was the mediator between the angel who spoke to him on the mountain and our fathers; it was he who was entrusted with words of life to hand on us. But our fathers did not want to listen to him, they rejected him and turned in their hearts towards Egypt, saying to Aaron: "Make for us divinities to go before us, because we do not know what has happened to this Moses who led us out of Egypt." And in those days they made a calf, and offered sacrifices to the idol, and they rejoiced over the work of their own hands (Acts 7:38-41).

In Exod. 32, no mention is made of a "turn toward Egypt": it comes, in fact, from Num. 14:4, in such a way that idolatry is connected to a nostalgia for Egypt that the Exodus account does not contain (the people demand a sign in order to proceed, not to go back). Aaron is saved from every charge. Consider the use of the verb *moschopoiein* ("make a calf"), a neologism that Christian apologetics will make great use of to accuse the Jews of zoolatry.[15] This term – and the intellectual travesty it indicated – and the fact that the "rejoicing" does not allude to any explosion of instincts, give, I think, this passage the tones of the sapiential polemic against idols. It suggests the incredible foolishness of those who give homage to an object they have themselves produced. The consequence of this perversion, more of the intellect than of the senses, is that God abandons his people to astral cults (Amos 5:25-27 is misread to this purpose).

Going on to the second part of the polemic, that against the Temple (Acts 7:48: the Highest do not live in material places!), we may note that from the two capital premises – idolatry and Temple: manipulation in a materialistic sense of the divinity, radical incomprehensions of Mosaic monotheism – comes the final invective, which takes over the prophetic and deuteronomic formula, "stubborn and uncircumcised in the heart and in the ears, you always resist the Holy Spirit: as were your fathers, so are you" (no longer "our" but "your"; the separation increases). Here, then, is the final charge. The Jews have persecuted and killed the prophets and have betrayed and killed the Righteous One. The execution of Stephen, who, immersed in his vision, dies giving pardon, immediately follows.

Different in literary tone, destination and content, Stephen's speech is the second important document in our New Testament dossier. The emphasis is different, compared to Paul. For Paul, it was "bad

---

[15]See Pelletier (1966).

Appendix I

desire," *epithymia-concupiscentia*; for Stephen it is intellectual perversion which presides over the materialization of the divinity. Different aspects of the antiidolatrous polemic applied to the Jews these may be, but they are not separable and are often historically intertwined.

3. Ancient Versions of Exodus 32:1-6

Among the ancient versions of Hebrew (the Masoretic text, referred to hereafter as M), the Targums (the paraphrastic Aramaic versions, which had a liturgical, synagogal use) have pride of place. For the text with which I have been concerned, we have above all the Targum Onqelos (O), the official canonic Aramaic version of the Torah, fairly faithful to the Hebrew, and which was adopted by the Babylonian Jews (it is for this reason that we call it the Babylonian Targum, despite its Palestinian origin). We can tentatively locate its final redaction between the years 70 A.D. and 135 A.D. As well as these texts, we have the Palestinian Targums, whose circulation was far more limited but whose interpretation was far freer. These include Targum Pseudo-Jonathan (PJ), Targum Neophyti (N), the fragmentary Targum (F). PJ, the most paraphrastic of all the documents, is the result of an evolution that reached its conclusion only in the seventh century; N, recently edited, and less free than PJ, can be placed in the second or third century.[16]

Before beginning a proper analysis, I propose a very literal translation of the broadest and most evolved text, PJ: a reading that may give some idea of Targumic methods of interpretation. The words in italics indicate the elaboration of the Targum; those between brackets belong to PJ rather than to N as concerns content. This is merely a simple expedient which has no claims to methodological rigor (it does not indicate what belongs to N), but I hope it will serve to reveal the process by which the paraphrase is amplified and how it gradually but increasingly assimilates diverse traditions (remember that O differs from the Hebrew M only slightly, as we shall see from the forthcoming analysis).[17]

---

[16] I refer above all, among the vast literature, to the work of Le Deaut (1966), and in particular to his *Targum du Pentateuche I: Genese* (SC 245, Paris (1966) pp. 15-73, and, for Exod. 32:1-6: to *Targum du Pentateuche II: Exode et Levitique* (SC 256, Paris 1979) ad loc.

[17] A very rigorous comparison between PJ and N in Le Deaut, *Targum du Pentateuche II* cit. ad loc. I use the following editions: for the Targum Onqelos, A. Sperber, *The Bible in Aramaic* (Leiden: 1959) and the translation by J.W. Etheridge, *The Targums of Onkelos and Jonathan ben 'Uzziel on Pentateuch, with the Fragments of the Jerusalem Targum* (1862-65; new ed. New York 1968);

1. And the people saw that Moses was tardy in coming down the mountain, and the people gathered around Aaron [when they saw that the time he had fixed for them had passed. And Satan came, and led them astray, and perverted their hearts with pride]. And they said: "Get up! Make us divinities to walk in front of us, because this Moses, the man who brought us from the land of Egypt, [has been consumed by the fire on the mountain that burns before the Lord] we do not know what has become of him."

2. And Aaron said to them: "Take off the rings of gold that your women, your sons and your daughters have on their ears and bring them to me."

3. [*And the women refused to give their ornaments to their men*] and then all the people took off the rings of gold that they wore on their ears and brought them to Aaron.

4. And he took (them) from their hands [*and wrapped them with a cloak*] *and threw them into the form* and made of it a golden calf. And they said: "Here are your *divinities*, Israel, that brought you out from the land of Egypt."

5. *And Aaron saw Hur* [*dead*] *before him, and was afraid,* and built another altar before him. And Aaron shouted [*with a pained voice*] and said: "Feast tomorrow before the Lord [*to make sacrificial offerings of these enemies that have denied the Lord and exchanged the glory of his shekinah for this calf*]."

6. And the following day they got up early and offered holocausts, and presented sacrifices, and the people sat down to eat and drink, and they rose to make revelry *licentiously in a foreign cult*.

Ignoring the numerous non-Targumic parallelisms, which would divert us away from our immediate purposes,[18] let us analyze the details of these and other ancient versions. Present here are also the Samaritan Targum, and more obviously the Septuagint, the Vulgate, the Syrian version (Peshitta), as well as the Arab version.

(V. 1) PJ expatiates on the notion of tardiness and the intervention of Satan. We have parallels for this in the rabbinic tradition, and I will return to these themes a little later.[19] "Divinity": O translates elohim as *dahalan*, an object to be venerated, an idol (arabic *ma`budan*). N does not translate, but recounts in Hebrew: "And they said: 'Get up! Make us elohim to walk before us.'" A marginal note: "one

---

for N A. Diez Macho, Ms *Neophyti 1, II Exodo* (Madrid and Barcellona 1970); for PJ: M. Ginsberger, *Pseudo-Jonathan nach Londoner Handschrift* (1903; new ed. Hildesheim and New York 1971).

[18] Useful in this sense, as well as Le Deaut, *Targum*, cit., ad loc., are Ginzberg, *Legends*, vol. 3, pp. 119-24 and vol. 6, pp. 51-53; Smolar and Aberbach (1968) pp. 91-116. Ginzberg's edition also contains a more reduced version of parallel passages.

[19] ExR 32, 1 (477); Shab 89a.

reads, one does not translate." A similar but not identical prescription is found in Mishnah (Meg.IV 10), which authorizes the translation of the entirety of Exod. 32:1-20, with the exception of the end (vv. 21-25 and 35).[20] Preserving it in the original text helps to maintain both the emotive and the historical distance from the episode. N and PJ: "we do not know what has become of him"; PJ allows the people to believe that Moses has been devoured by the divine fire. The Origenian *Hexapla* signals a variant in the column of the Septuagint: *aner* instead of *anthropos* as the appellation given to Moses (just as they signal, alongside *syneste, synathroisthe, epaneste* referring to the people "that they gathered in a meeting," heb. *yiqqahel*, aram. *'tknys*).[21]

(V. 2) The Septuagint omit "of your sons": can it not be said that men wear ear-rings? "According to the Arab custom," says one tradition.[22]

(V. 3) On the behavior of the women who refuse to take part in the idolatrous cult, there exists a misogynous Christian version, to which reference has been made earlier.[23]

(V. 4) The problem of how the golden calf was made. To the Hebrew *heret* O inserts *wsr ytyh bzyp'*, which Etheridge translates: "and formed it with a graver," thus preserving the ambiguity; N has *wrmh yth btwps'* (keeping the Hebrew in margin), as does PJ (and the Syrian version): "and he threw it into the form" (see *typos*). But PJ also adds another interpretation, "he wrapped it in a cloak." The Septuagint translate *eplasen auta en tei graphidi*, with a "stylus." The *Hexapla* propose, alongside *graphidi, en technei*. The Vulgate overcomes the problem by translating "formavit opere fusorio."[24]

(V. 5) N and PJ bring Hur into play. N: "He saw Hur the prophet before him" (in the margin: "He saw Hur sacrificed before him"); PJ: "He saw Hur put to death before him"; F: "He saw Hur, the son of his sister, killed before him." According to the Midrashic tradition, Hur was killed during a rising of the people. This tradition is taken over by Christian authors.[25] "And he was afraid," present in N, PJ and F, is passed on to the Syrian version. "He built an altar" – note that the term indicates the kind of altar used for the true cult, *mdbh*, like the

---

[20]See Le Deaut, *Targum* cit., *ad loc.*, note 2; Diez Macho, *Neophyti* cit., *ad loc.*, note 7; MacNamara (1978) pp. 48 ff.
[21]See *Origenis Hexaplorum quae supersunt*, F. Field ed. (1075; new ed., Hildesheim 1964) *ad loc.*
[22]Pirqe de Rabbi Eleazer, ed. G.Friedlander 45 (354).
[23]See Ginzberg, *Legends*, vol. 3, p. 121.
[24]See Le Deaut, *Targum*, cit., *ad loc.*, note 5.
[25]See ExR 38, 21 (571); 32, 7 (481): LvR 8, 1 (123); Sanh 7a; Pirqe de Rabbi Eleazer, ed. G. Friedlander 45 (353).

Septuagint *thysiasterion*, not *bomos*, with the same apologetic intent.[26] In the margin of N, Aaron's specific prayer is mentioned: "He made a proclamation and said: 'May it please heaven that the sacrifice is against me if there is the feast of the evil before God tomorrow.'" PJ, however, thinks of the future atrocity at the hands of the Levites, and recalls Ps. 105:20, of which I have spoken .

(V. 6): The unanimous insistence of N, F and PJ: "revel licentiously in the foreign cult," while the *paizein* of the Septuagint is more neutral.

In conclusion, the Jewish exegetic tradition, as it is reflected in the ancient versions, is motivated not only by the need to clarify obscure details (for example, how the golden calf is made, "revelry"), but also by the concern to address the question of the fundamental obscurities of the episode – the responsibilities of the people and of Aaron. Such responsibilities need to be defined, and Aaron exculpated. With the exception of Satan's role, and the refusal of the women (as well as the Levites), from the apologetic standpoint, the people are held responsible by the ancient translators. This standpoint becomes ever more evident during the evolution which amplifies and enriches the paraphrase. Aaron, who is saved, seeks to offer resistance in various ways, but is made victim of the events (above all of Hur's death).

4. The Golden Calf in the Koran

The episode of the golden calf appears in the Koran on many occasions (sura 2:54.92-93; 4:153; 7:148-53; 20: 83-98). In the context of this non-specialist appendix, whose purpose is to give information and favour the comparison of different traditions, I here propose sura 20:83-98. This is the broadest and perhaps the most ancient tradition of the episode, coming from the second Meccanite period, according to Regis Blachere[27] (before 616 A.D.). The other, briefer traditions are certainly Medinian (for sura 7:103-76, Blachere suggests the third Meccanite period).[28] Here is the passage which concerns us:

> 83. "And what has caused you to hurry away from your people, Moses?" 84. He answered: "They follow me closely and I have hurried

---

[26]See Le Deaut, *Targum*, cit., *ad loc.*, note 6, with further references.

[27]*Le Coran: traduction selon un essai de reclassement des surates* (Paris 1951) p. 179. The section of sura 20 with which I have been concerned comes later, according to R. Bell, *The Qur'an: Translated with a Critical Rearrangement of the Surah* (Edinburgh 1937, new ed. 1960) vol. 1, p. 293. In translating I sometimes followed Blachère or Bell, but mainly A. Bausani, *Il Corano*, Firenze, Sansoni, 1978.

[28]Ibid., p. 631.

to you, Lord, so that you may be pleased with me." 85. "Your people – He said – have been tested while you were away, and the Samaritan led them astray." 86. And Moses went back to his people full of anger and sadness and said: "My people! Did not the Lord make you a good promise? Did the time seem too long? Or do you want the anger of the Lord to be vent on you because you broke your promise to me?" 87. They answered: "We did not break the promise that we made of our own accord, but we were loaded with the burdens of people's ornaments, which we threw into the fire. The Samaritan also threw something into the fire." 88. And he made from the ornaments a calf for them, a body which produced a lowing sound. And they said to the people: "This is your god, the god of Moses, which he has forgotten." 89. Could they not see that it gave them no answer, and had no power to bring them harm nor good? 90. And Aaron had already said to them: "My people! You have been tested by this calf, but the Merciful one is your Lord: follow me and obey my orders." 91. They answered: "We shall not cease to worship it until Moses comes back." 92. And when Moses came back, he said to his brother: "Aaron, what hindered you, when did you see them go astray 93. from following me? Did you then disobey my command?" 94. "O son of my mother – he answered – do not seize me by my beard, nor by my hair! I was afraid that you would tell me: 'You have caused a division among the children of Israel and did not obey my word!'" 95. "And what do you mean to do, Samaritan?" 96. "I saw what they did not see, and I took a piece of earth from the footstep of the Messenger and I threw it into the fire. My mind thus commanded me." 97. Moses said: "Go away! Throughout your earthly life it will be your lot to say to those who approach you: 'Touch me not!' And in your other life there is a threat ready for you that you shall not escape." And now look at your god who you continued to worship devotedly. We shall burn it and scatter all the ashes in the sea! 98. Because your god is God, there is no other God than He, who embraces all things in his knowledge!"

Let me make one or two observations which draw on the reference to the parallel passages of the other suras. According to the Koran, the people follow Moses, who is forced to hurry in order to stop the people tramping over the sacred space of Mt. Sinai (see Exod. 19:21-24).[29] The people fail the test that the tardy Moses' absence had set them, and are corrupted by the Samaritan (*as-Samiri*, of whom more later).

The sin of the people is incredulity, their lack of faith in the "clear signs" it had received from the exodus: "Moses had brought you clear signs and you preferred the calf in his absence, you iniquitous ones!" (sura 2:92; see 4:153: "then they chose for themselves the calf, after they had received clear signs"). The sin, as in some Jewish traditions, is contemporaneous with the acceptance of the pact: "we listen but [literally 'and'] we rebel" (sura 2:93, which adds: "and they were in

---

[29]Ibid., p. 188.

their hearts permeated by the calf," a spiritual interpretation of the fact narrated in Exod. 32:20, while in sura 20:98 only the dispersion of the ashes is mentioned, as in Deut. 9:21).

Aaron's sin consists of not stopping the people, and on account of this he is the object of Moses' anger: "He took his brother by the head pulling him towards him. And Aaron shouted: 'O son of my mother! The people have humiliated me and were about to kill me.'" (sura 7:150: Jewish tradition). But above all there is the sin of the Samaritan. The people offer the material, the tokens, but it is to him that is owed the making of the calf, "a body which emitted lowing sounds," but does not speak and cannot guide the people (sura 7:148). In the introduction of a mysterious character, there is probably the original aetiological intention of tracing the ancient separation between Samaritans and Jews back to this figure and his sin.[30] More precisely, Speyer has suggested that behind the Samaritan one can see Zimri ben Salu, whose memory is condemned for idolatrous fornication in Num. 24:14.[31] Furthermore, he contextualizes the figure of the Samaritan in the background of the rivalry between Jews and Samaritans which appears in the New Testament (John 4:9; 8:48; Luke 10:30), and in the link that aprocryphal writings establish between Satan and the Samaritans. The contribution of the Samaritan to the sin of Israel consists in the use of satanic magic: he sees what the Israelites do not see and takes a fistful of earth from the footstep of the angel and throws it in the fire (sura 20:96: who is the angel? perhaps Gabriel, perhaps Moses himself). It is the Samaritan who makes the calf, but together, he and Aaron say (plural): "This is your God" (v. 88).

Over all, finally, prevails divine mercy, thanks to Moses' intercession: "In this way he pardoned them: in truth it is he who always pardons, the Benign one" (sura 2:54); "yet they even passed over this impiety" (sura 4:153).

---

[30]*Loc. cit.*
[31]Speyer (1931) pp. 329 ff. Speyer also cites the opinion of Horovitz (Koranische Untersuchungen, vol. 1, 1926, vol. 1, pp. 144 ff) according to which we should think of the "calf of Samaria" which Jeroboam raised.

Appendix II

Images and Stereotypes of the Jewish People in the Ancient World: Golden Ass, Golden Calf

From the earliest beginnings of the pagan anti-Jewish polemic[1] in the second century B.C., the parodies of Exodus have played an important role.[2] It is true that the milieux foreign or hostile to Judaism did not have first hand access to the biblical sources.[3] We must wait until the second century for Celsus, against whom Origen writes, to find a polemic which draws on correct and direct biblical quotations. It is probably also true that there is a "history of the impure," who contaminate Egypt and are expelled, a history more ancient than the specific anti-Jewish polemic. Its subsequent versions, quoted at the end of the first century, by Flavius Josephus in his *Contra Apionem* – namely, the version of Hecataeus of Abdera (beginning of 3rd century B.C.), the fuller version of the Egyptian priest Manetho (3rd century), of Chaeremon and of Lysimachus (both otherwise little known authors of the 1st century), and of Apion – with their gradual application to the Jews of that most ancient stereotype display a growing

---

[1] Two recent and wide-ranging syntheses: H. Conzelmann (1981) and J.N. Sevenster (1975), both of which have bibliographies and, furthermore, J.L. Daniel (1979) pp. 45-65. In my opinion, I. Heinemann (1931) remains among the most important contributions. Two Italian contributions: M. Adriani (1965) p. 63 ff and A.M. di Nola (1970) coll. 427-472. Concerning the ancient sources, to the collection edited by T.H. Reinach (1895) has been added the three volume collection by M. Stern (1974, 1980 and 1984) with introductions, translations, comments and bibliographies for each author. Hereon referred to as "Stern."

[2] For a few remarks see C. Levy (1979) pp. 51-79, especially p. 72.

[3] Cfr. A. Momigliano (1975).

accumulation of specific anti-Jewish traits, motivated by a generic xenophobia.[4] Finally, it is true that these stories not only contain polemic and scorn, they also contain more or less explicit recognition and appreciation of, above all, the high importance and purity of Moses and the Jewish cult. These moments of appreciation and recognition are clearly visible in the work of Hecateaus of Abdera, in what Strabo of Amaseia seems to borrow from Posidonius (about 135-51 B.C.), in the work Pompeius Trogus (1st century ad), and in Tacitus Cornelius' own nonetheless critical judgments.

However, these words of warning and caution should not prevent us from seeing what was obvious to Josephus when he collected all these histories in order to refute them. They draw their main meaning from their status as distortions or reversals of figures, facts, affirmations essential to the historical identity of the Jewish people. Basing myself primarily on Manetho (Josephus, C. Ap. 1, 227-287), I will attempt to list some of the motives that recur in these "tendentious" versions of Jewish history and, above all, in Exodus.

First, the descent of the Jews from the people of the shepherds, the Hyksos, the feared enemies and invaders of Egypt (this, in fact, suited Josephus insofar as he saw there some recognition of the antiquity of his people).

Second, we have the inversion of the boils episode, which is traced back to the impurity of the Jews. A pestilence invades Egypt, but it has been caused by the impure ones and the lepers who live there (Hecateaus of Abdera in Diodorus, Bibl. XL, 3). For Manetho, the presence of the impure race prevents the King from "seeing the divinity." According to Chaeremon, Isis appears in a dream to Amenhotep and reproaches him. As a result, the Pharaoh decides to expel the impure (C. Ap. 1, 289). According to Lysimachus (306) and Tacitus (Hist. V, 3), the oracle of Ammon warns the Pharaoh Bocchoris that the lepers and the impure must be expelled.

Third, in place of the call to Moses to free the people, the oracle to Pharaoh, which pleads that the impure be crushed.

---

[4]This is the argument followed by Heinemann (1931) p. 25 ff. For arguments concerning the inner workings of Egyptian culture, M.J. Yoyotte (1963) pp. 133-143. The discussion is further complicated by the interference brought by the inventions of Jewish apologetics, which aim at showing the dependence of Greek wisdom on Jewish knowledge. In the same way, the possible successive interpolations, as in Manetho for example, which have the purpose of accentuating or even creating an anti-Jewish tone in texts in which it would have otherwise been absent are also adumbrated. For my purposes, however, the question of attribution is not strictly relevant.

Appendix II

Fourth, Moses' origin is Egyptian, not Jewish. Indeed, in Manetho's account the figure of Moses is split in two, into the soothsayer and magician who foresees the disaster which the presence of the Jews brings and who shares the same name as the Pharoah, Amenhotep, and Osarsif, the leper priest of Eliopolis, who puts himself at the head of the rebellious people.[5]

Fifth, instead of the covenant with God and the pledge of faith in Moses, we have a conspiracy that commits the Jewish people to eschewing all contact with those who have not taken the same oath (Manetho, C. Ap. 1, 261): instead of God's love and love of one's neighbor, we encounter misanthropy, and this will appear again and again among the accusations.

Sixth, a Jewish plot commits the Jews not only to refusing the Egyptian cult of the animals, but also to destroying those animals in sacrifice. Manetho tells of incursions into the Temples and raids on sacred places. This charge of *hierosylia*, sacrilegious theft, could be an exaggerated echo of the theme of the consenting plundering of the Egyptians, narrated in Exod. 12. Lysimachus of Alexandria even glimpses here the origin of the name "Jerusalem" (C. Ap. 1, 311).

Seventh, instead of the miraculous crossing of the Red Sea, we read about how the lepers are drowned, on the command of the Pharoah, and how the other impure ones are abandoned in the desert, where they light fires during the night and fast religiously. An exhortation to Moses follows: "do not show mercy to anyone, follow only the worst advice and destroy all the sanctuaries and altars they might meet" on the road to Jerusalem (C. Ap. 1, 308-310).

All this may seem like a perverted reflection of the events narrated in Exodus, from the flight out of Egypt on. The expert eye might be able to glimpse in these accounts not so much alternative historical versions of Exodus (although this too is a "biased" account), as exemplary applications of the techniques of transformation, condensation and substitution that Freud found in the work both of the oneiric and in comic elaboration.[6]

---

[5]One of the signs which convinced the Pharaoh is the hand of Moses which can become "leprous, white as snow." In the translation of Exod. 4:6, the Seventy omit *metso'arah* (leprous), a sign perhaps of their concern for the bad use to which this episode could be put.

[6]In further reference to Freud's *Jokes and their Relation to the Unconscious* (1905) in which Judaism has so much importance, we may observe that we are not dealing here with the witty rejoinder internal to Judaism, but with a brutal joke, a sarcasm which supposes a complete extraneousness. If we wanted to recall the word game, remembered by Freud (*Jokes*, II, 3) which rests on the difference between "anti-Semitic" and "ante-Semitic" (the furious anti-

Is the asinine cult, the onolatry, falsely attributed to the Jews in different forms, one of the parodies of Exodus? To one who has studied with some care the anti-Jewish use to which Christians put the golden calf, that episode crucial for Jewish history, it seems logical to ask whether the charge of onolatry in the Hellenistic and Roman authors' anti-Jewish polemic is also contained in the disfigured memory of that fact. And I will attempt to answer my question. But first, let me repeat that in examining the dossier of these charges, my aim is not so much to show their more or less direct dependence on Exod. 32 as to establish a general comparison between two anti-Jewish stereotypes, the pagan and the Christian.[7]

Written testimony on ancient anti-Semitism is fragmentary. It originates in different places and at different times, is of varying reliability and importance, and so mediated that any attempt at unequivocal attribution is difficult. Indeed, it is impossible not only to draw out of these elements a complete picture, but also to define their underlying "essence" of ancient anti-Semitism. (By way of approximating the kind of difficulty encountered in using this limited and compromised evidence, I. Heineman has suggested that it equals the difficulty of researching the origins of the First World War using cuttings from the English newspapers of 1914).[8]

Yet, with this caveat in mind, let me add that in the totality of these uneven and often incoherent fragments, the news of the asinine cult is a relatively constant and common phenomenon.[9] Thus the cult deserved, and still deserves, special attention. It is mentioned for the first time by Mnasea of Patara, at Lycia, Asia Minor. Mnasea writes perhaps at the beginning of the 2nd century B.C. At the beginning of the 1st century A.D., Apion speaks of the cult at Alexandria, and Josephus

---

Semitism of those who want to deny their origins), we would also have a theory on the origin of the information concerning Judaism of which, despite everything, ancient pagan satire seemed to have knowledge. This is a theory destined to remain such, but which at all accounts shows the nature of not only the processes which are reflected in the materials of the kind I am concerned with but also the cognitive attitudes we must adopt when dealing with them.

[7]This has already been widely studied by E. Bickerman (1927 and 1980), who critiqued a nonetheless very useful essay by A. Jacoby (1927) pp. 2165-282. Bickerman's theses were received by Heinemann (1931). The texts can now be found in Stern, accompanied by copious annotations. A recently published essay, which has a great deal of historical-religious documentation is W. Fauth (1973) pp. 79-120. On Seth-Typhon, the monograph by H. Te Velde (1967) is very clear, especially p. 109 ff for remarks on anti-Semitism. On the symbolism of the ass, and on its ambivalence, cfr. N. Ordine (1987).

[8]Heineman (1931) col. 4.

[9]Sevenster (1975) p. 8.

Appendix II

traces the slander back to Apion's sources: the authoritative Posidonius and Apollonius Molon (1st century B.C.: Apollonius is the first author of a specific text against the Jews). Also in the 1st century B.C., Diodorus also refers to something similar, as we shall see. (Here again Posidonius has been taken as the source.) Tacitus makes reference in the *Historiae*, and Plutarch contributes useful information. Further, the slander appears among the Christians at the end of the 2nd century, as Tertullian, Minucius Felix and others tell.

We are dealing, then, with something that for three centuries circulates around the great areas where the often explosively violent conflict between Judaism and the contemporary religious and political powers is played out. It appears in the Syrian area (above all, the version of Mnasea, which perhaps came prior to the persecution of Antiochus Epiphanes); in the Egyptian area (in Apion, who at the time of the great tumults in Alexandria represented the Greeks before Caligula, while Philo pleaded on behalf of the Jews); in Rome. And there exists one more minor but nonetheless important center. This is Rhodes, where Apollonius Molon, and then Posidonius, lived and where their valued opinions attracted the visits of many illustrious Romans.

The history of the asinine cult, as it emerges from these sources, takes three shapes. First, according to Mnasea of Patara, in the Temple there was the head of a golden ass. But while a long war was being waged between Jews and Idumaeans, one of the latter tricked his way into the Temple of Jerusalem and stole the head (C. Ap. 1, 112-114). Apion's version is similar. He recalls Apollonius Molon and Posidonius, and declares that the Jews had placed the head of a golden ass in the Temple and worshipped it. This was made public, he adds, at the time of the plundering of the Temple at the hands of Antiochus Epiphanes. At that time, the very valuable golden head was uncovered (C. Ap. 11, 80). In a later passage, Apion recounts that the Jews practiced a form of ritual anthropophagy.[10]

Second, Diodorus (Bibl. XXXIV, 1,1-5), recounts that in the temple Antiochus Epiphanes found a statue of a bearded man sitting on an ass with a book in his hand.[11] Commentators have usually attributed this version to Posidonius.

---

[10] The same information – onolatry and ritual killing – is passed on by a certain Damocritus in a brief note (Stern, no. 247).

[11] The legend to which Plutarch refers can be connected to this information. The legend states that the enemy of Isis and the killer of Osiris, Typhon, escapes on an ass for seven days and, once saved, fathers two children, Ierosolymus and Iudaeus (De. Is. 31). I will return to this theme.

Third, as we find in Plutarch and Tacitus, the Jews worshipped the ass because it had allowed them to discover a source of water (Plutarch, Quaest. conv. IV, 5,2) and showed them the path in the desert (*"effigiem animalis, quo monstrante errorem sitimque depulerant, penetrali sacravere"* Tacitus, Hist. V, 4,1).

For over a century, the interpretation of this data, and its organization in a genetically plausible and coherent series has engaged the most talented scholars. By utilizing the results of this research and integrating them with one or two new elements or hypotheses, we may formulate the following sequence, which will allow us to follow the various stages of ancient anti-Semitism:

1. At the origin lies the story of a trick played by the Idumaeans on the Jews. (Who is really the most astute? Who is the real thief?) The Jews, believing they were cannier and hoping themselves to capture the effigies of their enemies' divinity, fall into the trap and allow themselves to be robbed of their own effigy, a ridiculous golden-headed ass. This story probably existed previously and is simply applied here to the Jews. It can be traced back at least to the wars in the Syrian-Palestinian territory of the fifth and sixth centuries between Jews and inhabitants of Edom. The source is Mnaseas of Patara (beginning of the second century).

2. The same story is once again exploited in Syrian-Palestinian milieux, and in the Seleucidic epoch, some ten decades later. According to Antiochus Epiphanes' anti-Jewish propaganda, it is not true that no image of God exists in the Temple, but it is true, as he himself was able to confirm on entering there, that an ass is worshipped. To this slanderous charge is added the charge of ritual murder by the Jews. This combination is intended to throw infamy onto the Jewish cult and to justify sacking the Temple (Apollonius Molon, beginning of 1st century B.C.).

3. When the news of the onolatry (which justifies the malicious curiosity felt over the mysterious nature of the Jewish cult), arrives in Egypt, perhaps by way of the Idumaeans who lived there, it is grafted onto the common and strongly xenophobic explanation of the Jewish presence in the country.[12] This explanation considers the Jews an impure people, thrown out into the desert and after many vicissitudes led by a priest into Palestine (thus previously Manetho). This parody of Exodus, of which much has been said, supposes, a superficial, if deformed, knowledge of the main Jewish historical events. Such as an Alexandrian might have had. Onto it is grafted the ass. In fact, the role of guide, in a moment of difficulty during the crossing of the desert,

---

[12]Stern I, p. 98.

Appendix II

is attributed to the ass. It is from here that Tacitus, and later Plutarch, draw their explanation of the Jewish cult of the ass (mentioned above).

At this point let me allow myself to wonder whether the worship of the golden calf plays a part in the distortions of Exodus? The starting point for the golden calf narrative is Moses' lack of guidance: the idol is whoever "brought the people out" and whoever "will walk at the head of the people," in the absence of Moses.[13] Although not necessary, but perhaps interesting, this conjecture serves to introduce a comparison that I will develop a little later and that will constitute this section's final point and conclusion.

4. Alongside the "ethnographic" version of the origins of onolatry, witnessed by Plutarch and by Tacitus (one of the many legends of help offered by animals to man), a mythology develops (also vouched for by Plutarch). It consists in the Jews-Seth link – in other words, the link to Typhon, the enemy of Isis and the killer of Osiris. This is an ancient association. According to Manetho, Avaris, the capital of the Hyksos, the forefathers of the Jews, is a "city consecrated to Typhon, according to ancient theology" (C. Ap. I, 238). And the association delimits the foreigner as such, according to information from Plutarch:

> [The Egyptians] believe that the ass owes its likeness [to Typhon] not only on account of his stupidity and lust, but also to the color of his skin. Thus, in their special hatred of Ochus among the Persian kings, as one accursed and polluted, they called him the ass, and he said: "This ass indeed will feast on your ox," and he sacrificed Apis, as Deinon says. But those who say that Typhon's flight from the battle was made on the back of an ass and lasted for seven days, and that after he had made his escape, he became the father of two sons, Hierosolymos and Iudaeus, are manifestly, as their very names show, trying to turn Jewish things into myth.[14]

---

[13]It could be conjectured that the calf could not remain such in the course of the deformation because it would have recalled the cult of Apis, thus causing the parody to fail. Furthermore, "Apis is the living image of Osiris" (Plutarch, De Is. 43), and, based on what I will say later on the association between Jews and Seth, the enemy of Osiris, the bovine image could not be used.

[14]De Is. 31. Stern, I, p. 563, and Griffith (1970) p. 418 f.

We can see in this passage the condensation of many images[15] and especially of Seth (translated by the Greeks as Typhon).[16] Seth is "the enemy of the goddess (Isis), horrendously bloated on account of the deceits of ignorance"; he kills Osiris (De Is. 2), and, finally, is defeated by Isis who resuscitates her son. But "Typhon's evil power, even if weakened and partly consumed, is engaged once more in a final fight against death" (De. Is. 30). His Egyptian name, Seth, means "he who opposes" or "he who wreaks violence" (ibid. 41). The aridity, the wind, the sea, the darkness. Typhon is not only all this. Rather, he is everything of danger and destruction that Nature holds (ibid. 45). Typhon represents that part of the vital breath which is subject to the passions, deprived of order and intelligence, titanic and inconstant: in the physical structure of the universe, Typhon is the mortal component, cunning and infected, like seasonal anomalies, inclement weather, the darkening of the sun and the disappearance of the moon, all things which reveal Typhon's attacks and attempts at rebellion. The name that Typhon is given, Seth, means just this: it indicates at one and the same time something that wreaks tyranny, which imposes itself with force and also something which changes and twists continuously and which transgresses the law (ibid. 49). "For the Egyptians, everything that is essentially ignoble and dangerous – animals, plants, happenings – is work, part and manifestation of Typhon" (ibid. 50). "We must simply attribute to Typhon everything of these elements [water, sun, earth, sky] that stretches beyond the right measure, beyond the established order, both in excess and in defect" (ibid. 64).

We may notice from De Is. 31 how the ass-Typhon association is established through his "stupidity and sexual incontinence."[17] The inhabitants of Coptus have the custom of smashing an ass by dropping it down from on high because Typhon was red-faced and had the skin of an ass. "For the Egyptians, the ass is an impure and demonic animal, given its likeness to Typhon" (ibid. 30); "among domestic animals, they place alongside him [Typhon] the most stupid, the ass, and among the

---

[15]Fauth (1973) p. 115. He identifies the combination of many traits: a) Seth's flight pursued by the victorious Horus, Typhon's flight pursued by Zeus and Israel's flight from Egypt; b) the Seth/ass parallels, Moses riding an ass and the arrival of the Messiah on an ass; c) the symbolism of the Jewish week, the role of the seventh God (Sabaoth-Saturn) in Hellenistic astromagy; d) the cults of the local Baal and the interpenetration of cult of Seth and Western semitic cults; e) the sacral role of the ass in the wandering of Israel in the desert.
[16]Greek mythology, Typhon is a dragon who has been born of Era at Delphi, and is fought by Zeus and Apollo.
[17]Also found in the Bible: "licentious like asses" (Ezek. 23:20).

Appendix II

wild animals the most ferocious, the crocodile and the hippopotamus" (ibid. 50).

Furthermore, we see in De. Is. 31 that the ass-Typhon link had previously been applied to a despised Persian by the name of Artaxerse III Ochus, who had deified the ass.[18] The Egyptian hatred for the great Persian kings was enormous, and tradition attributed to Cambises and Ochus, as it had done previously to the Hyksos, the worst crimes (massacre of sacred animals, violation and sacking of Temples and burial grounds). The invading Persian armies, however, found in the Jewish colony in Egypt elements who were willing to collaborate,[19] as had happened previously with the Roman invader. This must have been a cause of great tension among the nationalist and traditionalist ranks and the Jewish community, whose origins had previously been associated with the Hyksos in the account given by Manetho.

Finally, and most importantly, we learn from Plutarch's text of the existence of a tradition which makes of Typhon the progenitor of the Jews. Here, after a seven-day flight on an ass he fathers Hierosolymus and Iudaeus, the eponymous forefathers of the Jewish city and the nation.[20]

We find here a mythical elaboration of Antiochus Epiphanes' version of Jewish origins and desecration (which we found also in Diodorus and which was attributed to Posidonius). This is clearly the Egyptian version – the history of the "impure" – which is completed with the mention of the statue of Moses on the ass:

> Antiochus [VII Sidetes, about 130] was laying seige on Jerusalem: the Jews resisted until, their provisions exhausted, they were forced to move the cessation of the hostilities. Most of his friends advised him to take the city by force and completely eradicate the race of the Jews (*to genos arden anelein ton Ioudaion*): because they, alone among others, refused to have any relation with any other people and considered them all enemies. They informed him that the forefathers of the Jews, impious and hated by the gods, had been expelled from all of Egypt. Covered in white spots and leprosy, constituting a curse, they were gathered together and thrown beyond the confines of the country in order to purify it. The expelled ones had taken control of the territory of Jerusalem and, forming the people of the Jews, had made a tradition of their hatred for men: for this reason, they had introduced absolutely outlandish laws: do not sit at table with foreigners, show them no good will. The friends of the king reminded him of the ancient hatred of his forefathers for the Jews. Antiochus, called Epiphanes, on defeating the Jews had gone into the part of the

---

[18]Cfr. Stern I, p. 98. Also De Is. 11.
[19]Yoyotte (1963) p. 140 ff.
[20]Hopfner (1941) p. 143 ff and Griffiths (1970) p. 418 ff.

sanctuary of their God where only the priest is permitted to go. He had found a statue in stone of a bearded man sitting on an ass with a book in his hands. He had thought that it was the image of the founder of Jerusalem and the organizer of the nation, he who had imposed on the Jews their misanthropic and lawless customs (*ta misanthropa kai paranoma ethe*). Antiochus, struck by this misanthropy toward all peoples, decided to abolish their institutions (Hist. XXXIV, 1,1-3).

Whether or not Posidonius is Diodorus' actual source,[21] the symmetry between the two passages is evident (note the parallelism between Hierosolymus and Iudaeus, the two sons, "the founder of Jerusalem and the organizer of the nation"), just as it is evident that both accounts come from Egyptian anti-Semitic milieux. We have already noted that Plutarch makes reference to this, without agreeing to it, as is also the case with the mythical version of Jewish history.[22]

The mythical image of Seth dominates that of the legislator of the abominated people; it is the source of its interpretation, its revelation. Behind the figure of Moses, behind the people, behind its institutions, there lies the dark shadow of Seth, a figure we must understand in all the radical negativity that traditonal identification with the Greek Typhon was not fully able to achieve. Greek syncretism tends to lessen the danger represented by Seth, the evil and destructive duplication of his brother Osiris who assails and threatens as the desert and the sea surround the strip of fertile land along the Nile.

With this mythical background in mind, it is easier for us to understand how the first authentically anti-semitic proposal to "totally destroy the race" came about. Anti-Semitism presupposes a radically negative opinion which invests the very being of the hated people and not its historic itinerary. It necessarily brings with it a destructive instance, even if historical circumstances do not necessarily permit the execution of that instance.

---

[21]The question can never probably be solved. Cfr Stern I, p. 143 and p. 184. Cfr also Gager (1972) p. 124 ff. Note that Diodorus (or Posidonius) does not share the advice of the "friends" of King Antiochus VII: the story ends by recounting how "being magnanimous and of mild nature," he does not listen to the most serious charges and does not issue orders to destroy the city, but limits himself to knocking down the walls of Jerusalem.

[22]"They try, as is evident from the very names they use [Ierosolymus and Iudaeus], to turn Jewish things into myth," *ta ioudaika parelkondes eis mython*, as if, known to all the facts (the expulsion of the people and the flight of Moses for seven days on an ass, the foundation of Jerusalem and the organization of the people), the myth of Typhon had been illegitimately applied: but Plutarch ignores Egyptian anti-Semitism and does not understand the pertinence of the association between Seth and the Jews (see also the conjecture which seems to induce him to place Judaism among the Bacchic cults (Quaest. conv. IV, 6).

Appendix II

The symbolism of the ass, then, beneath its apparent ludic nature, points to serious dangers and deep threats. Bearing in mind what has here been outlined, we can better understand the seriousness that underpins the imaginative playfulness of the story of Lucius. In the story as it is told by Apuleius, after being turned into an ass, Lucius is redelivered as a man thanks to the mediation of Isis. Turning to the Roman milieux, we can also better understand why Tacitus, who was so hostile to the Jews and was the first to underline their profanity with his news of the consecration of a statue of an ass in the Temple (and, as an offence to Ammon and Apis, of sacrifices of rams and oxen), begins his presentation of Jewish customs in terms of an inversion of the sacred and the profane ("Moses...introduced new rituals, contrary to those of other mortals. Everything that is sacred for us, there is profane, and what we abhor, there is allowed to them" [Hist. V, 4, 1]). We also understand much better the seriousness carried by the insult of the caricature of the crucified slave with an ass' head and the anti-Christian slander reported by Tertullian (Ad nat 1, 144; Apol. 16) and by Minucius Felix (28, 7). We have a new understanding of Epiphanes' assertion that some gnostics believed the archon Sabaoth, the creator of the world, had the form of an ass (the priest Zechariah, again according to the gnostic source, discovers that in the temple an asinine figure was worshipped, but before he can warn the Jews he is killed).[23] Gnosis, then, seems to be the extreme heir to pagan anti-Semitism and takes over the figure of the ass to express the radical dualism between the good divinity of the New Testament and the evil version of the Jews.

Paradoxically, we have thus far hardly glimpsed the golden calf in our attempt to define its role in the parodies of Exodus in the Hellenistic-Egyptian environment. But as I have made clear, it was not so much this hypothesis that interested me as the possibility of establishing parallels between the two figures. And we have seen how the episode of the calf is considered by Jewish tradition as the "closest Jewish equivalent to the concept of Christian original sin," and how, for its part, the Christian anti-Jewish polemic takes over the episode.

At this point, and making our way towards a conclusion, we can introduce the comparison between the charges: onolatry and idolatry. The difference is clear. Onolatry is a charge leveled from without by paganism against monotheism in an attempt to embarrass monotheism by revealing its inner contradictions. The charge of idolatry comes from within; it is leveled by a variant of monotheism on its main and most

---

[23]The most documented and complex essay on these developments is by Fauth (1973). A shorter source is the article *onos* edited by O. Michel in TWzNT V, 283-288.

ancient branch. But what is the common element of these two charges? Both perceive danger in the not unjustified claim that the mysterious Jewish cult enjoys greater antiquity and spirituality. Consider this: the first contacts Hellenism made with Judaism are marked by a series of admiring recognitions, as is testified by the texts of Theophrastus, Clearchus of Soli, Megasthenes and Hecateaus of Abdera.[24] And Christianity, quite rightly, drew from Jewish Scripture, which it could never renounce, the uneasy certitude that the the Jewish people was its older brother, even if the younger had been preferred by God, as with Jacob at Esau (Rom. 9:11). Thus, for the pagans and the Christians, reminding their brother of the ridiculous and humiliating cult allowed them to reveal, behind Judaism's claim of greater spirituality, its authentic face, its dullness, sensuality, aggressiveness. These emerge clearly from the cult of the ass, with everything the symbol represents. And the traits of "carnality," which are exemplified by the episode of idolatry, reemerge in all Jewish history up to the killing of Jesus.

But the same critical operation – the denigration of a threateningly superior figure – took on a different value for pagans and Christians respectively. The pagan polemic is born of a perception of difference from Judaism. Consider: the norms which govern food and marriage, as well as those concerning worship (the ban on images, the non-participation in "normal" religious life)[25] created a perception of separateness between pagans and Jews. The pagans, from their perspective, justified it by postulating an original impurity in the Jews and imputing to Moses the elaboration of a code of behaviour hostile to every other people. The same *humanitas*, the same stoic universalism of Posidonius and Seneca were challenged by the exclusiveness of some Jewish attitudes. Despite the efforts made by the Jewish-Hellenistic apologists, it was difficult for them not to see this most glaring contradiction with the higher values that late-ancient popular philosophy was then spreading. Onolatry symbolically condensed the instinctive baseness and danger of Jewish ideology. In the mythical Hellenistic-Egyptian universe, where it is amplified by its link with Seth-Typhon, the charge ended up by locating Judaism at that polar point to which all the negativity of existence was attracted. Anti-Semitism and its subsequent program of destruction consists of a dualism

---

[24]Cfr. Momigliano (1975) ch. IV.

[25]The accusations of an economic nature, which were to become so important later, are almost entirely non-existent: this is also the case for many centuries in Christian milieux. (I know of no case in the first millenium in which the golden calf episode is used to level a charge of this kind. Later it will be massively exploited.)

Appendix II 113

which attributes to the enemy characteristics of absolute negativity. That the ancient world was able to elaborate definitions which mythically concentrated absolute negativity in Judaism seems to me by now clear. Given the scarcity of information, we cannot draw a complete or certain picture of the diffusion and depth of penetration of these extremist formulations. Such definitions, however, circulated at crucial moments and points. It seems correct to add that goodwill toward the classic world often obstructs our reading and prevents us from evaluating with sufficient severity the anti-semitic attitudes that were certainly to its fore, even if they did not necessarily result in destructive explosions.[26]

---

[26] I take the opportunity to point out (and concur with) a recent work conducted from a different perspective, J-L. Daniel (1979) p. 64 ff: "The frequency (and intensity) of the disparaging remarks justifies the conclusion that anti-Semitism was more deeply ingrained and more widespread than many modern scholars allow. Anti-Semitic remarks range all the way from incidental mentions in the papyri to carefully composed statements in serious histories. It was not necessarily a virulent anti-Semitism; certainly not (except on occasion) persecution, but rather an enduring contempt, coupled with distrust."

Abbreviations

CC	*Corpus Christianorum* (Turhout and Paris 1953 ff.)
CSCO	*Corpus Scriptorum Christianorum Orientalium* (Paris 1903 ff.)
CSEL	*Corpus Scriptorum Ecclesiasticorum Latinorum* (Wien 1866 ff.)
ExR	*Midrash rabbah, Exodus,* tr. H. Freeman and M. Simon, in *Midrash rabbah,* 10 vols., London 1939
Philo, Oeuvres	*Les oeuvres de Philon d'Alexandrie,* edd. R. Arnaldez, J. Pouilloux and C. Mondésert (Paris, 1961 ff.)
GCS	*Die griechischen christlichen Schriftsteller der ersten drei Jahrhunderte,* Leipzig 1897 ff.
GnR	*Midrash rabbah, Genesis,* quoted as ExR
Ginzberg, Legends	L. Ginzberg, *The Legends of the Jews,* 7 vols., Philadelphia 1909-46
IDB	*The Interpreters Dictionary of the Bible,* New York and Nashville, A1962 ff.
LvR	*Midrash rabbah, Leviticus,* quoted as ExR
MEW	K. Marx and F. Engels,*Werke,* Berlin 1961 ff.

MGH	*Monumenta Germaniae Historica*, Hannover and Berlin, 1826 ff.
NmR	*Midrash rabba, Numbers*, quoted as ExR
PG	*Patrologia Graeca*, ed. J. P. Migne, Paris 1857-66
PL	*Patrologia Latina*, ed. J. P. Migne, Paris 1844-55
PLS	*Patrologia Latina, Supplementum*, ed. A. Hamman, Paris 1958 ff.
PO	*Patrologia Orientalis*, ed. R. Graffin and F. Nau, Paris 1903 ff.
PS	*Patrologia Syriaca*, ed. R. Graffin, Paris 1894 ff.
RACh	*Reallexikon für Antike und Christentum*, Stuttgart 1941 ff.
SC	*Sources Chrétiennes*, Paris 1942 ff.
Stern	Stern M. (ed.), *Greeck and Latin Authors on Jews and Judaism*, Jerusalem, 1974, 1980 and 1984.
ThWzNT	*Theologisches Wörterbuch zum Neuen Testament*, ed. G. Kittel and F. Gehhardt, Stuttgart 1932 ff.
WA	*Martin Luthers Werke, Weimarer Ausgabe*, Weimar 1883 ff.

Bibliography

Aberbach A. e Smolar L., "Aaron, Jeroboam and the Golden Calves," in *Journal of Biblical Literature*, 86 (1967), 129-40.
Adriani M., "Note sull'antisemitismo antico," in *Studi e materiali di storia delle religioni* 36 (1965), 63 ff.
Auzou G., *De la servitude au service* (Paris: Ed. de l'Orante, 1961).
Aziza C., *Tertullien et le judaïsme* (Paris: Les Belles Lettres, 1977).
Bailey L.R., "The Golden Calf," in *Hebrew Union College Annual*, 42 (1971), 97-115.
Barth K., *Die kirchliche Dogmatik*, 4, 1 (Zürich: EVZ Verlag, 1953).
Beyerlin W., *Herkunft und Geschichte der ältesten Sinaitraditionen* (Tübingen: Mohr, 1961)
Biblia patristica: index des citations et des allusions bibliques dans la littérature patristique, Centre d'Analyse et de Documentation patristique de (Strasbourg-Paris: Ed. du C.N.R.S., 1975 ff.).
Bickerman E., "Ritualmord und Eselskult," in *Monatschrift für Geschichte und Wissenschaft des Judentums*, 1927, now in *Studies in Jewish and Christian History*. Leiden: Brill, 1980, 225-255.
Bietenhard H., "Deuterosis, " *RACh*, 3 (1957), 842-57.
Blanchetière F., "Aux sources de l'antijudaisme chrétien," in *Revue d'Histoire et de Philosophie religieuses*, 53 (1973), 354-98.
Blumenkranz B., *Die Judenpredigt Augustins: ein Beitrag zur Geschichte der jüdisch-christlichen Beziehungen in den ersten Jahrhunderten* (Basel, 1946, Paris, 1973).
--*Juifs et chrétiens dan le monde occidentale*, 430-1096 (Paris-La Haye: Mouton, 1960).
--*Les auteurs chrétiens latins du Moyen Age sur les juifs et le judaïsme* (Paris-La Haye, 1963).

Bori P.C., "Una pagina inedita di Freud: la premessa al romanzo storico su Mosè," in *Rivista di Storia contemporanea*, 8 (1979), 1-17, now in *L'estasi del profeta* (Bologna: Il Mulino, 1989), 237-258.

--"The Church's Attitude towards the Jews: an Analysis of Augustine's Adversus Judaeos," in *Miscellanea Hist. Eccl.* 6 (1982), 301-311, now ibid., 119-130.

--*Il vitello d'oro. Le radici della controversia antigiudaica* (Torino: Boringhieri, 1983).

--*L'interpretazione infinita. L'ermeneutica cristiana antica e le sue trasformazioni*, Bologna, Il Mulino, 1987.

--*Immagini e stereotipi del popolo ebraico nel mondo antico: Asino d'oro, vitello d'oro*, in *Ebraismo e antiebraismo: immagine e pregiudizio*, Firenze, Giuntina, 1989, 149-160, now in *L'estasi del profeta*, 131-150.

Bori P.C.-Bettiolo P., *Movimenti religiosi in Russia prima della Rivoluzione, 1900-17* (Brescia: Queriniana, 1978).

Bovon F., *Luc le théologien* (Neuchâtel-Paris: Delachaux et Niestlé, 1978).

Cassuto U., *A Commentary of the Book of Exodus* (1951) (Jerusalem: The Magnes Press, 1974).

Cazelles H., *A la recherche de Moïse*. (Paris: Ed. du Cerf, 1979).

Childs B.S., *The Book of Exodus* (Philadelphia: Westminster Press, 1974).

Coats G.W., *Rebellion in the Wilderness* (Nashville-New York: Abingdon Press, 1968).

Conzelmann H., *Heiden, Juden, Christen, Auseinandersetzungen in der Literatur der hellenistisch-romischen Zeit* (Tübingen: Mohr, 1981).

Daniel J.L., "Anti-semitism in the Hellenistic-Roman Period," in *Journal of Biblical Literature* 98 (1979), 45-65.

Deconinck D., *Essai sur la chaine de l'Octateuche* (Paris: H. Champion, 1912).

De Lange N.R.M., *Origen and the Jews: Studies in Jewish-Christian Relations in Third-Century Palestine* (Cambridge: Cambridge U.P., 1976).

Nola A.M., " Antisemitismo," in *Enciclopedia delle religioni* 1 (1970), 427-472.

Efroymson D.P., "Tertullian's Anti-Judaism and Its Role in His Theology, "diss. Temple University, Philadelphia, 1975.

Fauth W., "Set-Typhon, Onoel und Eselsköpfige Sabaoth. Zur Theoriomorphie der orphitisch-barbelognostischen Archonten," in *Oriens Christianus* 57 (1973), 79-120.

Fensham F.C., "The Burning of the Golden Calf and Ugarith," in *Israel Exploration Journal*, 16 (1966), 191-93.

Feuerbach L.A., *Das Wesen des Christentums* (1841) (Berlin: Akademie Verlag, 1973).
--Freud S., *Jokes and their Relations to the Unconscious* (1905) in *The Complete Psychological Works of Sigmund Freud*, J. Strachey ed. (Toronto: Hogarth Press), vol. 6.
--*Moses and Monotheism: Three Essays* (1938), in *The Complete Psychological Works of Sigmund Freud*, J. Strachey ed. (Toronto: Hogarth Press), vol. 23.
Gager J.G., *Moses in Greco-Roman Paganism* (Nashville-New York: 1972).
Gelsi G., *Kirche, Synagoge und Taufe in den Psalmenhomilien des Asterios Sophistes* (Wien: VWGÖ, 1978).
Grego I., *La reazione ai giudei-cristiani nel quarto secolo negli scritti patristici e nei canoni conciliari* (Jerusalem: Franciscan Printing Press, 1973).
Griffiths J.G., *De Iside et Osiride* (Cardiff: Univ. of Wales Press, 1970).
Hahn J., *Das 'Goldene Kalb': die Jahwe-Verehrung bei Stierbildern in der Geschichte Israels* (Fränkfurt-Bern: P. Lang, 1981).
Hegel, *Die Positivität der christlichen Religion*, in *Hegels theologische Jugendschriften* (Tübingen 1907; anast. repr. Frankfurt a.M.: Minerva, 1966).
Heinemann I., "Antisemitismus," in Pauly-Wissowa-Kroll, *Realencyclopädie der classischen Altertumswissenschaft*, 5 (1931), 3-43.
Hopfner T., *Plutarch über Isis und Osiris*, II (Prague 1941; repr. Hildesheim-New York: Olms, 1974).
Hruby K., *Juden und Judentum bei den Kirchenvatern* (Zürig: Theologischer Verlag, 1971).
Hvidberg-Hansen O., "Die Vernichtung des Goldenen Kalbes und der Ugaritische Ernteritus," in *Acta orientalia*, 33 (1971), 5-46.
Jaros K., *Die Stellung des Elohisten zur kanaanäischen Religion* (Göttingen: Vandenhoek u. Ruprecht, 1974).
Jacoby A., "Der angebliche Eselskult der Juden und Christen," in *Archiv für Religionswissenschaft* 25 (1927), 265-282.
Judant D., *Judaïsme et christianisme: dossier patristique* (Paris: Ed. du Cèdre, 1969)
Juster J., *Les juifs dans l'empire romain: leur condition juridique, économique et sociale* (Paris: 1914; repr. New York, Burt Franklin, s.d.).
Le Déaut R., *Introduction à la littérature targoumique* (Roma: Pontificio Istituto Biblico, 1966).
Lehming S., "Versuch zu Exodus 32," in *Vetus Testamentum*, 10 (1960), 16-50.

Lestienne M., "Dieu se repent: Exode 32, 7-14," in *Christus*, 89, n. 23 (1967), 94-105.

Levy C., "L'antijudaïsme païen: essai de synthèse," in *De l'antijudaïsme antique à l'antisémitisme contemporain*, ed. V. Nikiprowetzky (Lille: Presses Universitaires, 1979), 51-79.

Lewy I., "The Story of the Golden Calf Reanalyzed," in *Vetus Testamentum*, 9 (1959), 318-22.

Loewenstamm S.E., "The Making and Destruction of the Golden Calf," in *Biblica*, 48 (1967), 481-90.

--"The Making and Destruction of the Golden Calf: a Rejoinder," in *Biblica*, 56 (1975), 330-43.

Lubac H. de, *Exégèse médiévale: le quatre sens de l'Ecriture* (Paris: Aubier, 1959-64).

MacNamara M., *The New Testament and the Palestinian Targum to the Pentateuch* (Rome: Pontifical Biblical Institute, 1978).

Malingrey A.M., "La controverse antijudaique dans l'oeuvre de Jean Chrysostome d'après les discours de l'Adversus judaeos,'" *De l'antijudaïsme antique à l'antisémitisme contemporain*, ed. V. Nikiprowetzky (Lille: Presses Universitaires, 1979), 87-104.

Marthelet G.,"Sacrements, figures et exhortation en 1 Cor. 10-1-11," in *Recherches de Sciences religieuses*, 44 (1956), 323-59, 515-59.

Martin-Achard M. (ed.), *La figure de Moïse* (Genève: Labor et Fides, 1978).

Marx K., *On the Jewish Question* (1843), in *Karl Marx: Selected Writings*, ed. David McLellan (Oxford: University Press, 1977).

Meeks W.A. and Wilken R.L., *Jews and Christians in Antioch in the First Four Centuries of the Common Era* (Missoula: Scholars Press, 1978).

Momigliano A., *Alien Wisdom. The Limits of Hellenization* (Cambridge: Cambridge U.P., 1975).

Moore G.F., "Christian Writers on Judaism," in *Harvard Theological Review*, 14 (1921), 197-254.

Neusner J., *Aphrahat and Judaism: the Christian-Jewish Argument in Forth Century Iran* (Leiden: Brill, 1971).

Noth M., *Ueberlieferungsgeschichte des Pentateuchs* (Stuttgart, Kohlhammer, 1948).

--*Das zweite Buch Mose* (Göttingen: Vandenhoek u. Ruprecht, 1958, 5th ed. 1973).

--"Zur Ausfertigung des Goldenen Kalbes," in *Vetus Testamentum*, 9 (1959), 419-22.

Ordine N., *La cabala dell'asino. Asinità e conoscenza in Giordano Bruno* (Napoli: Liguori, 1987).

Pelletier A., "Une création de l'apologétique chrétienne: 'moschopoiein,'" in *Recherches de Sciences religieuses*, 54 (1966), 411-16.
Perdue L.G., "The Making and Destruction of the Golden Calf: a Reply," *Biblica*, 54 (1973), 237-46.
Petuchowski J.J., *Vetus Testamentum*, 10 (1960), 74.
Poinsotte J.M., *Juvencus et Israel: la représentation des juifs dans le premier poème latin chrétien* (Paris: P.U.F., 1979).
Prigent P., *Les Testimonia dans le christianisme primitif: L'Epître de Barnabé 1-16 et ses sources* (Paris: Gabalda, 1961).
Quasten J., *Patrology* (Utrecht-Westminster (USA): Spectrum-Christian Classics, 1950-1986).
Rad G. von, Theologie des Alten Testaments, 2 vols. (München: Kaiser Verlag, 1965-66).
Reinach Th., *Textes d'auteurs grecs et romains relatifs au judaïsme* (Paris: 1895; repr. Hildesheim: Olms, 1963).
Ritter A.M., "Erwagungen zum Antisemitismus in der Alten Kirche: Johannes Chrysostomos," in *Bleibendes im Wandel der Kirchengeschichte*, ed. B. Moeller and G. Ruhrbacht (Tübingen: Mohr, 1979), 71-91.
Ruether R.R., *Faith and Fratricide: the Theological Roots of Anti-Semitism* (New York: The Seabury Press, 1979).
Sanders E.P., *Paul and Palestinian Judaism: a Comparison of Patterns of Religion* (London: S.C.M. Press, 1977).
Sasson J.M., "Bovine Symbolism in the Exodus Narrative," in *Vetus Testamentum*, 18 (1968), 380-87.
Schmid H., *Mose: Ueberlieferung und Geschichte* (Berlin: A. Töpelmann, 1968).
--*Die Gestalt des Mose. Probleme alttestamentlicher Forschung unter Berücksichtigung der Pentateuchkrise*, Darmstadt, Wiss. Buchgesellschaft, 1986.
Schmidt H.A.P., *Hebdomada sancta* (Rome, Freiburg-Barcelona: Herder, 1956-57).
Schneider G., *Die Apostelgeschichte*, 1 (Freiburg, Basel - Wien: Herder, 1980).
Schreckenberg H., *Die christlichen Adversus-Judaeos-Texte und ihr literarisches und historisches Umfeld (1.-11.Jh.)* (Frankfurt a. M.-Bern: P. Lang, 1982).
Sevenster J.N., *The Roots of Pagan Anti-Semitism in the Ancient World* (Leiden: Brill, 1975).
Sgherri G., *Chiesa e Sinagoga nelle opere di Origene* (Milan: Vita e Pensiero, 1982).

Simon M., *Verus Israel: étude sur les rélations entre chrétiens et juifs dans l'empire romain, 135-425* (Paris, 1948, 2nd ed. Editions du Boccard, 1964).

--*St. Stephen and the Hellenists in the Primitive Church* (London: Longmasn-Green, 1958).

Simonetti M., "'Per typica ad vera': note sull'esegesi di Ireneo," in *Vetera christianorum*, 18 (1981), 357-82.

--"L'interpretazione patristica del Vecchio Testamento," in *Augustinianum*, 22 (1982), 7-33.

--*Lettera e/o allegoria. Un contributo alla storia dell'esegesi patristica* (Roma, Inst. patristicum "Augustinianum," 1985).

Smolar L. and Aberbach M., "The Golden Calf Episode in Postbiblical Literature," in *Hebrew Union College Annual*, 39 (1968), 91-116.

--"Golden Calf," in *IDB* suppl. (1976) 123 sg.

Speyer H., *Die biblischen Erzälungen im Qoran* (1931) (Hildesheim: Olms, 1961).

Steck O.H., *Israel und die gewaltsame Geschick der Propheten* (Neukirchen - Vluyn: Neukirchener Verlag, 1967).

Stern M. (ed.), *Greek and Latin Authors on Jews and Judaism*, 3 vols. (Jerusalem, Israel Academy of Sciences and Humanities, 1974 ff).

Te Velde H., *Seth, God of Confusion. A Study of his Role in Egyptian Mythology and Religion* (Leiden: Brill, 1967).

Troeltsch E., "Was heisst 'Wesen des Christentums,'" (1903) in *Gesammelte Schriften* (Aalen: Scientia, 1961-62).

Valentin H., *Aaron: eine Studie zur vor-priesterlichen Aaron-Ueberlieferung* (Göttingen: Vandenhoek u. Ruprecht, 1978).

Walzer M., "Exodus 32 and the Theory of Holy War: the History of a Citation," in *Harvard Theological Review*, 61 (1968), 1-14.

Wengst K., *Tradition und Theologie des Barnabasbriefes* (Berlin-New York: W. de Gruyter, 1971).

Wilde R., *The Treatment of the Jews in the Greek Christian Writers of the First Three Centuries* (Washington: The Catholic University of America, 1949).

Wilken R.L., *Judaism and the Early Christian Mind: a Studi of Cyril of Alexandria's Exegesis and Theology* (New Haven-London: Yale U.P., 1971).

Williams A.L., *Adversus Judaeos: a Bird's Eye View of Christian Apologiae until the Renaissance* (Cambridge: Cambridge U.P., 1935).

Yoyotte M.J., "L'Egypte ancienne et les origines de l'antijudaïsme," in *Revue de l'histoire des religions* 82 (1963), 133 ff.

Index

Aaron 1, 2, 4, 5, 7, 9, 13, 15, 17-22, 34, 36, 38, 39, 57, 64, 68, 69, 71, 77, 85-91, 94, 96, 98-100

accommodation 32, 47, 48, 50, 51, 75

Adam 11, 12, 16, 25, 59, 77

African 32-34, 50, 77

anti-Semitic, anti-Semitism 13, 103, 104, 106, 110-113

Antiochus 59, 105, 106, 109, 110

Antiochus Epiphanes 105, 109

Apis 38, 66, 67, 77, 90, 107, 111

apostasies 74

apostasy 2, 4, 37, 44, 45, 51, 56, 73-74, 86, 88

ascetic, asceticism 55, 59

ass 13, 101, 104-112

Augustine 20, 24, 25, 35-37, 40, 47, 50, 53, 65, 67, 77, 79, 82

Barnabas 43, 51

Basil 37, 56, 58, 59, 77, 79

Bible 3, 4, 12, 33, 37, 38, 74, 76, 80, 90, 95, 108

biblical 2, 7-10, 13, 14, 17, 19, 21, 23, 27, 29, 37, 46, 56, 57, 66, 67, 73, 79, 83, 85, 90, 101

calf, calves 1-4, 8, 10, 12-21, 23-25, 29-31, 33, 35-40, 43-45, 50, 52, 53, 57, 62, 65-68, 73, 76-78, 85-91, 94, 96-101, 104, 107, 111, 112

carnality 7, 25, 27-29, 32, 34, 36, 38, 41, 50, 56, 59, 76-78, 80, 83, 112

Christ 11, 17, 23, 24, 27-29, 40, 44, 51, 52, 55, 56, 65, 67, 75, 79, 80, 82, 83

Christian 3, 6-8, 11, 13, 14, 17, 19, 21, 23-25, 27-29, 32, 34-36, 38, 39, 42, 43, 45, 46, 50, 52, 53, 55, 56, 62, 65, 66, 73, 74, 76-81, 83, 86, 91-94, 97, 104, 111, 112

Christian Scripture 74, 92

Christianity 6-8, 16, 19, 28, 37, 41, 42, 46, 47, 71, 73, 74, 76-83, 112

Chrysostom, John 16, 19, 20, 34, 37, 39, 40, 46, 56, 58, 59, 61, 65-67, 77, 79, 81

Church 7, 8, 15, 17, 24, 33, 43, 44, 48-50, 55, 58, 64, 67, 72-75, 79, 80

communion 1, 11, 19, 55

Covenant 2, 10, 14, 15, 43, 44, 51, 73, 74, 76, 85, 86, 89, 90, 103

Creation 11, 20, 21, 30, 34, 41, 68, 71, 88

Cyprian 15, 34, 36, 39, 64, 74

Cyril of Alexandria 17, 19, 30, 34, 38, 50, 61, 66, 76

decalogue 3, 10, 11, 44, 48

Deuteronomy, Deut. 33, 37, 40, 43, 47, 53, 62, 68, 72, 90, 91, 100

documentary theory 86, 87

Egypt 1, 9, 15, 17, 19, 25, 29-31, 37, 38, 45, 46, 48, 86, 91, 94, 96, 101-103, 106, 108, 109

Egyptian 5, 22, 29, 31, 36, 38, 57, 58, 77, 87, 101-103, 105, 108-110

Epistle 43, 51, 73, 76

exegesis 2, 19, 20, 30, 38, 51, 58, 62, 76, 82, 86, 93

Exodus, Exod. 1, 7, 9, 10, 12, 13, 15, 19-22, 25, 29, 31, 33, 35-41, 43, 44, 47, 48, 52, 53, 55, 59-62, 64-66, 68, 71-73, 75, 79, 82, 85-88, 90-95, 97, 99, 100-104, 106, 107, 111

Faith 11, 15, 22, 35, 43, 46, 57, 58, 60, 65, 67, 82, 93, 99, 103

Flavius Josephus 13, 18, 101, 102, 104

flesh 7, 16, 27-29, 34, 41-43, 70, 71, 76, 78, 79, 82, 83, 93

flesh/spirit duality 27, 29

Freud, Sigmund 5, 6, 7, 103

God 1-6, 9-11, 14-16, 19-21, 23-25, 27-34, 36-38, 40, 41, 43, 45-49, 51-53, 56-58, 61, 66-72, 75, 79, 81, 83, 85, 86, 89-94, 98-100, 103, 106, 108, 110, 112

golden ass 101, 105

golden calf/calves 3, 4, 8, 10, 12, 13, 15-17, 23-25, 31, 35, 38, 43-45, 50, 53, 57, 65-67, 73, 76, 78, 85, 87-90, 96-98, 101, 104, 107, 111, 112

Hellenistic 11, 28, 55, 63, 104, 108

Holy Spirit 21, 74, 94

idolatrous 9, 10, 12, 14, 16, 17, 19-21, 24, 25, 31, 32, 36, 39, 40, 46, 50, 55, 66, 69, 71, 74, 76-78, 90-93, 97, 100

idolatry 3, 7, 9-12, 15-17, 20, 21, 25, 29-34, 36-38, 40, 41, 43-45, 48, 55-60, 63, 65-72, 75, 77, 80, 83, 90, 91, 93, 94, 111, 112

Islam, Islamic 3, 74, 81

Israel 1-3, 6, 9, 12-18, 25, 28, 32-35, 37, 40, 45, 46, 50, 52, 59, 67, 73, 74, 77, 79, 80, 86, 87, 93, 96, 99, 100, 108

Israelites 1, 2, 22, 43, 58, 61, 79, 100

Jacob 7, 15, 32, 40, 61, 73, 112

Jerome 35, 38-40, 57, 60, 61, 67, 70, 77, 79

Jesus 11, 15-17, 27, 30, 36, 43, 44, 56, 65, 74, 80-83, 94, 112

Jew 13, 16, 17, 36, 37, 41

Jewish 4, 6, 7, 9-12, 18-21, 23-25, 27, 28, 31, 32, 34-38, 40-43, 45-48, 50, 58, 59, 61, 62, 64, 73-78, 80-83, 90, 91, 98-104, 106-112

Jewish Scripture 37, 74-76, 81, 112

Judaism 6, 7, 12-14, 16, 25, 32, 33, 36, 41, 47, 52, 59, 71-83, 91, 93, 101, 103, 105, 110, 112, 113

Justin 15, 32, 37, 40, 48, 52, 75

Koran 23, 37, 47, 85, 98, 99

law 3, 5, 10-12, 16, 24, 27, 28, 32, 37, 42-53, 57, 65, 67, 74-76, 79, 83, 108

lusus 33, 60-63, 77, 79

Luther 38, 41, 56, 58, 67-72, 83, 93

Mediation 3, 45, 48, 111

Index

Mishnah 13, 97

monotheism, monotheistic 3-6, 9-11, 27, 56, 65, 80, 81, 94, 111

Moses 1, 2, 4-7, 9, 12-15, 17-19, 21-23, 25, 31, 32, 35, 37, 40-43, 45, 49-53, 55-58, 64, 65, 67, 72, 73, 77-79, 82, 83, 85-88, 90, 91, 94, 96-100, 102, 103, 107-112

Mt. Sinai 9, 14, 38, 40, 42, 51, 57, 60, 61, 77, 99

mystic, mysticism 3, 4, 11, 55, 82, 83

Nehemiah 31, 37, 90, 91

New Testament 3, 21, 28, 36-38, 40, 50, 53, 74, 82, 92, 94, 100, 111

Numbers, Num. 12, 37-39, 58, 82, 88, 93, 94, 100

Old Testament 2, 11, 38, 45, 52, 75, 80-82, 85, 92

onolatry 8, 104-107, 111, 112

Origen, Origenian 16, 36, 37, 39, 45, 47, 51-53, 57, 58, 66, 70, 74, 76, 79, 81, 82, 96, 101

original sin 9, 11, 12, 25, 59, 111

originary idolatry 29, 75

Osiris 105, 107, 108, 110

Paul 11, 22, 27-32, 42, 49, 51, 52, 57, 59, 66, 67, 70, 73, 75, 77, 82, 83, 92-94

Paul's 15, 24, 29, 30, 36, 37, 44, 52, 55, 56, 68, 69, 71, 77, 80

Philo 13, 18, 31, 38, 56, 58, 79, 82, 105

Psalms, Ps. 17, 22, 24, 29, 34-40, 61, 65-67, 90, 93, 98

redemption 6, 11, 14, 49

Resurrection 11, 27

Revelation 11, 110

revelry 2, 12, 17, 31-33, 50, 57, 59-61, 86, 89, 93, 96, 98

Samaritan 23, 96, 99, 100

Satan 14, 23, 31, 96, 98, 100

Scriptures 6, 43, 45, 47, 69, 73, 76, 81

Seth 107, 108, 110

sin 6, 9-13, 15-17, 19, 21, 22, 25, 34, 36, 46, 48, 52, 59, 63, 66, 68, 69, 71, 77, 79, 82, 86-88, 90, 91, 93, 99, 100, 111

spirit 7, 13, 21, 27-29, 34, 51, 52, 62, 69, 70, 74, 78, 79, 81, 83, 94

spiritual 6, 7, 24, 27, 28, 36, 43, 49, 51-53, 55, 59, 65, 67, 70, 71, 74, 76, 80, 82, 83, 100

spiritualism 81, 83

spirituality 6, 7, 28, 34, 38, 41, 56, 76-79, 112

Stephen 14, 24, 28, 29, 37, 38, 48, 74, 77, 92-95

tablets 1, 2, 5, 13-15, 24, 43, 46, 48, 49, 51-53, 58, 85, 90

Temple 5, 13, 28, 94, 105, 106, 111

Tertullian 15, 32-34, 37, 39, 40, 45, 56, 57, 61, 74, 79, 105, 111

Testament 2, 3, 11, 21, 28, 36-38, 40, 45, 50-53, 74-76, 80-82, 85, 92, 94, 100, 111

Torah 5, 12, 46, 95

Typhon 105, 107-110

Western 4, 22, 34, 39, 59, 108

South Florida Studies in the History of Judaism

240001	Lectures on Judaism in the Academy and in the Humanities	Neusner
240002	Lectures on Judaism in the History of Religion	Neusner
240003	Self-Fulfilling Prophecy: Exile and Return in the History of Judaism	Neusner
240004	The Canonical History of Ideas: The Place of the So-called Tannaite Midrashim, Mekhilta Attributed to R. Ishmael, Sifra, Sifré to Numbers, and Sifré to Deuteronomy	Neusner
240005	Ancient Judaism: Debates and Disputes	Neusner
240006	The Hasmoneans and Their Supporters: From Mattathias to the Death of John Hyrcanus I	Sievers
240007	Approaches to Ancient Judaism: New Series Volume One	Neusner
240009	Tradition as Selectivity: Scripture, Mishnah, Tosefta, and Midrash in the Talmud of Babylonia	Neusner
240011	In the Margins of the Midrash: Sifre Ha'azinu Texts, Commentaries and Reflections	Basser
240014	Understanding the Rabbinic Mind: Essays on the Hermeneutic of Max Kadushin	Ochs
240016	The Golden Calf and the Origins of the Jewish Controversy	Bori/Ward